Anonymous

Is there any Resemblance between Shakespeare & Bacon?

Anonymous

Is there any Resemblance between Shakespeare & Bacon?

ISBN/EAN: 9783337058357

Printed in Europe, USA, Canada, Australia, Japan

Cover: Foto ©ninafisch / pixelio.de

More available books at **www.hansebooks.com**

Is there any Resemblance

BETWEEN

Shakespeare & Bacon?

All the world's a stage,
And all the men and women merely players.—*Shakespeare.*

Modern play acting is but a toy, except when it is too biting and satirical.—*Bacon.*

Love is not love
Which alters when it alteration finds,
Or bends with the remover to remove.
O, no! it is an ever fixed mark
That looks on tempests and is never shaken.
It is the star to every wandering bark,
Whose worth's unknown, although his height be taken.
Love's not Time's fool, though rosy lips and cheeks
Within his bending sickle's compass come,
Love alters not with his brief hours and weeks,
But bears it out even to the edge of doom.—*Shakespeare.*

You may observe that amongst all the great and worthy persons (whereof memory remaineth, either ancient or recent) there is not one that has been transported to the mad degree of love, which shows that great spirits and great business do keep out this weak passion.—*Bacon's Essay on Love.*

1888.

LONDON:
Field & Tuer, The Leadenhall Press, E.C.
Simpkin, Marshall & Co.   Hamilton, Adams & Co.

COPYRIGHT SECURED IN ENGLAND AND AMERICA.

THE LEADENHALL PRESS,
LONDON, E.C.
T 4,354.

COPYRIGHTED
AT WASHINGTON, U.S.A.,
BY
CHARLES F. STEEL.
1888.

PREFACE.

THE following pages are not written with the expectation of affecting the attitude of those who from some unexplained animus desire to dethrone Shakespeare and to enthrone Bacon; neither are they expected to interest (although it is hoped they may) those who think this subject undeserving of serious thought. There is, however, a very large number whose doubts have been awakened, and who are honestly interested, to whom much that directly concerns this inquiry may not be easily accessible; to those the matter here presented, and the conclusions drawn, may be acceptable.

The endeavour has been to present such points as appeal to reason and common sense, though they have not been elaborated to the breadth that might be given them; the facts in themselves are convincing to unpartisan judgment, and need very little in the shape of argument to emphasize their force.

Bacon and his biographers are freely quoted in order to show that in every quality he was the opposite of Shakespeare, that he never did anything except for profit, or for fame and personal aggrandisement, and that he would not have devoted his time to bestow any of its productions upon the world without recognition or reward.

It is shown that Bacon had neither the fancy to create the sentiment, the poetic fervour to inspire the language, the heart to feel the truth and beauty, nor the generosity to deny himself the authorship of such plays; and that absolutely no grounds existed for concealment of poetic genius that would have promoted the object of his ambition; that he distrusted the permanency of the English language, disparaged the stage, condemned as wasted the time spent on fiction and works of the imagination, spoke contemptuously of love, and sneered at lovers: subjects that are the idols of Shakespeare's constant muse.

Examples are cited of verses that Bacon *did write and publish*, which his historians speak of as "flat effects," "bad lines," "ridiculous failures," and "low order," but which his present champions studiously ignore.

In the lifetime of these two men, one by the "sweetness of his nature" and his "uprightness of dealing" won the love of his friends and fellows, while the other by his "coldness of heart and meanness of spirit" drew upon himself general contempt and hatred. Now, after three centuries, a number of people appear who seem to delight in defaming the better and lauding the worse. They invent situations, invest historical characters with prejudices contrary to the facts, endeavour to discover imaginary hidden meanings, and aimless, mysterious motives; and one has quite outstripped all others by constructing an arithmetical vagary, crazy enough to set bedlam in ecstacy, in order to prove Bacon's genius and inclination to have been what every fact in his life, naturally, and logically, disproves.

By whatever extraordinary devices they strive to influence opinion, in so far as their efforts invite a study of Bacon, the friends of Shakespeare should wish them all success, for in that will be found one of the most effective refutations of their claim.

CONTENTS.

CHAPTER I.   PAGE.
Bacon's pride in his writings and their competency as testimony—General ignorance concerning him and his works—His 104th Psalm—His biographers' opinions of his attempts at versification—Contrast of his usual laborious method with the ease and freedom with which he must have "tossed off" Shakespeare's poems   9

CHAPTER II.
Repugnance to the Baconites' claim—Queen Elizabeth's estimate of Bacon—His doubt of the permanency of the English language—His quotations—His opinion of stage acting—His Essay on Masques and Triumphs—Ben Jonson's description of Shakespeare's strolling company   36

CHAPTER III.
The stage as a symbol—Shakespeare—Bacon—Bacon's notes on conversation—Hamlet's advice to the players—Bacon's apparatus of rhetoric—The Epitaph—Bacon's Tomb—The Cipher—The proclivities of Shakespeare and Bacon—Bacon as an Inquisitor—The quality of mercy—Bacon as a friend—Bacon's grants of patents to monopolies—Macaulay's estimate of Bacon's character—His servility to Buckingham—His pamphlet in favour of religious war—His falsification of history—Fairness of authorities quoted   66

CHAPTER IV.
Bacon as a "soaring angel"—Advice to the person who has incurred the displeasure of his prince—Thrift that follows fawning—Extracts from various essays—Essay on the True Greatness of Kingdoms—His attitude toward the civilization of his time   107

CHAPTER V.

Bacon's interpretation of "A just man is merciful to his beast," etc.—His essay on Deformity—His interpretation of another proverb—His habit of generalization—His Essay on Friendship—Mode of treatment for the human mind—His Essay on Love—His corpuscular study of Cupid 126

CHAPTER VI.

The New Atlantis—Bacon's sketch of Queen Elizabeth—His censure of fictions of the imagination—His resolve to publish all his writings—Time occupied in writing the plays—The Sonnets—Queen Elizabeth's dislike to Bacon—His propensity to borrow—His lack of traits that are glorified by Shakespeare 157

CHAPTER VII.

Court favourites as patrons of the stage—Shakespeare's industry and property in the plays—Bacon's manuscript—Bacon's experiment with the fowl—Bacon's whereabouts when the plays were collected—Adverse criticism upon Shakespeare—The classics—Bacon and the poem of Lucrece—The Promus ... 195

CHAPTER VIII.

What is known of Shakespeare's life—The burning of the Globe Theatre—Friendship between Lord Southampton and Shakespeare a deadly peril to Bacon—Play of Richard II. final and conclusive proof that Bacon had no connection with Shakespeare or the plays 245

CHAPTER IX.

Further defence of the Baconite claim impossible—Reasons for belief in Shakespeare—Ben Jonson's sketch of Shakespeare—Record proving authenticity and genuine work of the first editors—The man who stood near the king 268

CHAPTER I.

Bacon's pride in his writings and their competency as testimony—General ignorance concerning him and his works—His 104th Psalm—His biographers' opinions of his attempts at versification—Contrast of his usual laborious method with the ease and freedom with which he must have "tossed off" Shakespeare's poems.

IF Lord Bacon could have foreseen that at some future time a dispute would arise concerning him, and especially as an author, he would have rested in entire security, to have his writings speak for him, and it is largely with the view of presenting him by his own testimony that this volume is undertaken.

That he wished to be judged by his literary work cannot be doubted, and I am confident that by applying this rule it will appear that the fame he desired, and laboured to earn, was of a totally different nature from that which his admirers of the present wish to secure for him.

Probably no other writer, of any period, placed a higher valuation on his own works, gave more undisguised evidence of complete satisfaction with the result of his labours, or was more studiously economical of his time and of his genius. This characteristic is not only in striking contrast with Shakespeare, who absolutely ignored his own personality in his art, but it also lessens the possibility of Bacon having neglected or disowned any of the products of his thought. As illustrative of the estimate he placed on his works, and upon himself, the following is one of his introductions:

"Francis of Verulam's

GREAT INSTAURATION.

ANNOUNCEMENT OF THE AUTHOR.

"Francis of Verulam thought thus, and such is the method which he determined within himself, and which he thought it concerned the living and posterity to know."

He nowhere conceals his concern as to the place he shall occupy in history, or his anxiety as to how posterity shall judge him, and to secure for himself preëminent fame he spent untold time and labour upon the works that came from his hand. His "Novum Organum" was revised and copied twelve times before he gave it to the public, and he is said to have had it under reflection forty years. As evidence of the same nature, the following passage by Joseph Devey, M.A., in his introduction to Bacon's works, shows the author's solicitude for their preservation :

"The fate of Chaucer haunted him. He thought that modern languages would play the bankrupt with books ; and if he did not enshrine his thoughts in a dead language, his name would never travel abroad, and would positively die out among his own countrymen in the next generation. With the assistance of Herbert, Playfair, and some add Ben Jonson, he gave his new treatise, together with his essays and many of his minor pieces, a Latin dress; but on contrasting those works with the Novum Organum, originally written by him in Latin, it does not appear that he was much indebted to the attainments of his translators."

Macaulay says of him, "In his will he expressed with singular brevity, energy and pathos a mournful consciousness that his actions had not been such as to entitle him to the esteem of those under whose observation his life had been passed, and at the same time a proud confidence that his writings had secured for him a high and permanent place among the benefactors of mankind."

The high estimate that he placed upon his writings, and the care with which he prepared them, make them most competent testimony in a case of comparison. They go much further than that, however. They define his character, tastes, and opinions with such emphasis, repetition, and uniformity, as to place them in a speaking attitude toward every phase of the Shakespeare controversy.

What "Francis of Verulam thought," and what it now concerns posterity to know of the stage, of fiction, works of the imagination and of love, is expressed in such pronounced and careful manner in his writings as to leave no doubt as to his position upon, and relation to these subjects, which occupy so large a field in Shakespeare's life and genius. Bacon's expressions upon these subjects always indicate an inborn antagonism, instead of a resemblance, to Shakespeare, and it is probable that the result of the claim now made for him will be to diminish the reputation that he might have retained if undisturbed, for, in general, it rests largely upon the fact of his books being so little read. They have been relegated to remote places in libraries, and the popular idea of what they contain is to a great extent suppositious. It may be safely said that his works contain many surprises for those who have formed opinions of their contents from other sources than reading what he has written.

His reputation exists now, upon a preconceived idea of his mind, taste, and character. This is the case to that extent that one finds numbers of people who readily admit that they know little or nothing of him themselves, that they have not read his books; yet they are willing to admit the probability of his having written Shakespeare's marvellous works, simply from a vague impression of the universal nature of his acquirements.

I have thought that perhaps this easy admission, of what seems to me to be without a single fact or probability to support it, might be owing to a belief that the voluminous character of his writings makes it difficult to decide, without great labour, as to his poetic and dramatic talent. This is certainly an error. His metaphysical and legal works are entirely irrelevant to this subject, except as showing the nature of the study to which he devoted himself. His speculative works are not at all bulky, and are too positive to permit more than one interpretation of his attitude toward the stage and the drama. His faith in himself is too firm to allow any doubts to enter his mind in regard to the subjects which concern this inquiry, consequently his opinions are expressed in a manner not easily misunderstood. To discover what manner of man he was does not require much speculation, analysis, or sharpness of intellect; for one can judge, with far greater confidence, of the probabilities and possibilities of a nature that is fixed, dogmatic, and matter-of-fact than of a tolerant, imaginative, and subtle mind and disposition. In addition to his own writings we have the opinions of his historians and critics and history furnishes facts in his political career that have an important bearing upon his relation to the plays.

Hume says of him, "Most of his performances were composed in Latin; though he possessed neither the elegance of that nor his native tongue. If we consider him merely as an author and philosopher, the light in which we view him at present, though very estimable, he was yet inferior to his contemporary Galilæo, perhaps even to Kepler. Bacon pointed out at a distance the road to true philosophy; Galilæo pointed it out to others, and made himself considerable advances in it. The Englishman was ignorant of geometry; the Florentine revived that science, excelled in it, and was the first that applied it, together with experiment, to natural philosophy. The former rejected, with the most positive disdain, the system of Copernicus; the latter fortified it with new proofs, derived both from reason and the senses. Bacon's style is stiff and rigid. His wit, though often brilliant, is also often unnatural and far fetched, and he seems to be the original of those pointed similes and long-spun allegories which so much distinguish the English authors."

If I do not underrate the general acquaintance with Bacon's writings, his versification of a number of psalms will be new to a great majority of readers. As they are the only verses that he ever acknowledged or published, it would seem as though an honest desire to compare his productions with those of Shakespeare, would have given them the most prominent place in this discussion. It needs no argument to demonstrate the suitableness of Bacon's verses, rather than his prose, for comparison with Shakespeare, neither will it require any argument after reading them to explain the reason why they do not appear in the Baconite's exhibits. The longest and most descriptive of these attempts at versification is the 104th psalm :

"Father and King of powers, both high and low,
  Whose sounding fame all creatures serve to blow ;
  My soul shall with the rest strike up thy praise,
  And carol of thy works and wondrous ways.
  But who can blaze thy beauties, Lord, aright ?
  They turn the brittle beams of mortal sight.
  Upon thy head thou wearest a glorious crown,
  All set with virtues, polished with renown :
  Then round about a silver veil doth fall
  Of crystal light, mother of colors all.
  The compass heaven, smooth without grain or fold,
  All set with spangs of glittering stars untold,
  And striped with golden beam of power unpent
  Is raised up for a removing tent.
  Vaulted and arched are his chamber beams
  Upon the seas, the waters, and the streams :
  The clouds as chariots swift do scour the sky ;
  The stormy winds upon their wings do fly.
  His angels spirits are that wait his will,
  As flames of fire his anger they fulfill.
  In the beginning with mighty hand,

He made the earth by counterpoise to stand ;
Never to move, but to be fixed still ;
Yet hath no pillars but his sacred will.
This earth, as with a veil, once covered was,
The waters overflowed all the mass :
But upon his rebuke away they fled,
And then the hills began to show their head ;
The vales their hollow bosoms opened plain,
The streams ran trembling down the vales again ;
And that the earth no more might drowned be,
He set the sea his bounds of liberty ;
And though his waves resound, and beat the shore,
Yet it is bridled by his holy lore.
Then did the rivers seek their proper places,
And found their heads, their issues, and their races ;
The springs do feed the rivers all the way,
And so the tribute to the sea repay :
Running along through many a pleasant field,
Much fruitfulness unto the earth they yield :
That know the beasts and cattle feeding by,
Which for to slake their thirst do thither hie.
Nay desert grounds the streams do not forsake,
But through the unknown ways their journeys take :
The asses wild that hide in wilderness,
Do thither come, their thirst for to refresh.
The shady trees along their banks do spring
In which the birds do build, and sit, and sing ;
Stroking the gentle air with pleasant notes,
Plaining or chirping through their warbling throats.
The higher grounds, where waters cannot rise,
By rain and dews are watered from the skies ;
Causing the earth put forth the grass for beasts,
And garden herbs served at the greatest feasts ;
And bread, that is all viands firmament,

And gives a firm and solid nourishment;
And wine, man's spirits for to recreate;
And oil, his face for to exhilarate.
The sappy cedars, tall like stately towers,
High-flying birds do harbor in their bowers:
The holy storks that are the travellers,
Choose for to dwell and build within the firs;
The climbing goats hang on steep mountain's side;
The digging conies in the rocks do bide.
The moon, so constant in inconstancy,
Doth rule the seasons orderly;
The sun, the eye of the world, doth know his race,
And when to show and when to hide his face.
Thou makest darkness that it may be night
When the savage beasts that fly the light,
(As conscious of man's hatred) leave their den,
And range abroad secured from sight of men.
Then do the forests ring of lion's roaring
That ask their meat of God, their strength restoring;
But when the day appears, they back do fly,
And in their dens again do lurking lie.
The rolling seas unto the lot doth fall
Of beasts innumerable, both great and small.
The fishes there far voyages do make
To divers shores their journey they do take.
All these do ask of thee their meat to live
Which in due season thou dost give
All life and spirit from thy breath proceed.
Thy word doth all things generate and feed,
If thou withdrawest it, then they cease to be,
And straight return to dust and vanity.
The earth shall quake if aught his wrath provoke;
Let him but touch the mountains, they shall smoke.
As long as life doth last I hymns will sing

With cheerful voice to the eternal King.
I know that he my words will not despise,
Thanksgiving is to him a sacrifice.
But as for sinners, they shall be destroyed
From off the earth ; their places shall be void.
Let all his works praise him with one accord ;
Oh, praise the Lord, my soul ; praise ye the Lord ! "

Lest it may be supposed that these rhymes were produced in Bacon's youth, at a stage of life before such almost superhuman perceptions as Shakespeare's could develop, it must be stated that they were written some years after Shakespeare's death, about the time that Heminge and Condell were collecting and publishing the folio of 1623 under difficulties so well known, and when the author of the plays, if living, could have rendered such valuable services. These two of Shakespeare's fellow actors say in their preface, "It had bene a thing, we confesse, worthie to have bene wished, that the Author himselfe had liv'd to set forth, and overseen his owne writings ; but since it hath been ordain'd otherwise, and he by death departed from that right, we pray you do not envie his Friends, the office of their care, and paine, to have collected and published them ; and so to have published them ; as where (before) you were abus'd with divers stoln, and surreptitious copies, maimed, and deformed by the frauds and stealthes of injurious imposters, that exposed them: even those, are now offer'd to your view cur'd, and perfect of their limbs and all the rest, absolute in their numbers, as he conceived them. Who, as he was a happie imitator of nature was a most gentle expressor of it. His mind and hand went together; and what he thought, he uttered with that eassiness, that wee have scarce received from him a blot in his papers, . . . but collected them and done an office to the dead to procure his Orphanes, Guardians, without ambition either of self-profit, or fame; only to keepe the memory of so worthy a Friend and Fellow alive, as was our Shakespeare, by humble offer of his playes to your most noble patronage."

In 1624 Bacon dedicated his versification of the psalms to his friend Herbert, and published it. Can anyone imagine the author of the plays busy on such uncouth compositions at any time, particularly under circumstances which suppose Shakespeare's friends the victims of such pitiful deception? It is doubtful if Bacon ever occupied the attention of these two men, but it is impossible that he could have been ignorant of the work they were doing, especially if he had ever been interested in the plays; he undoubtedly read their preface. The absurdity does not end there, however, for Ben Jonson also wrote a long eulogy of Shakespeare in the preface to the same edition, besides his lines on the portrait, both of which have become immortal. Ben Jonson was closely intimate with Bacon, and it surpasses belief that this publication, or Jonson's connection with. it and his laudation of Shakespeare, could have been unknown to, or even unread by Bacon. Years after Bacon's death Jonson wrote again, in the "Discoveries," his sketch of Shakespeare, in which he refers to what the players often said of the great bard, quoting a part of their preface. Consider, then, what easy credulity is required to believe in the Baconite proposition.

The players must be imposed upon by their friend during a lifetime of most intimate association and co-labour. They must have been left in ignorance of his true character at his death. Ben Jonson must be either the dupe of both Bacon and Shakespeare, or in the scheme with them and lending his active aid to the deception. Can anyone imagine such an association? There is no warrant in Jonson's character, nor any act of his life, to support such theories. He prided himself upon honesty and "candour"; he was an actor and dramatist who felt no shame of his profession, and instead of joining Bacon to conceal such gifts, would have resented any insinuation that their exposition was not an enforced condition of possession, concealment irrational, paltry, and inconsistent with the profundity of wisdom to which Bacon aspired. No one who has read Ben Jonson will believe that he was a party to an imposition based upon the disgrace of his calling, nor will anyone believe that when he told "posterity" about Shakespeare and what the players said about him, (Shakespeare and Bacon were then dead) he was writing a carefully prepared falsehood. Purposeless and ridiculous as such suppositions would appear, they are not as strong an argument against the Baconite theory as the versification of the psalms. Spedding, of Trinity College, is one of Bacon's most partial historians, and it is interesting to know what he, as one of his friendliest critics, thinks of Bacon in this department of literature. He says, "The translation of certain psalms into English verse are the only verses certainly of Bacon's making that have come down to us, and probably with one or two exceptions are the only verses he ever attempted." This historian goes on then to say that he has "watched Bacon's progress in versification" and that the "effect of the two first experiments is flat enough," but as he advances, although there is an inevitable loss of lyric fire and force, this is compensated by "the development of meanings," etc. Again he says: "In compositions upon which a man would have thought it a culpable waste of time to bestow any serious labour, it would be idle to seek either for indications of his taste or for a measure of his powers."

And again: "Of these verses of Bacon's it has been usual to speak not only as a failure, but as a ridiculous failure: a censure in which I cannot concur. An unpractised versifier, who will not take time and trouble about the work, must of course leave many bad verses; for poetic feeling and imagination, though they will dislike a wrong word, will not of themselves suggest a right one that will suit metre and rhyme; and it would be easy to quote from the few pages, not only many bad lines, but many poor stanzas."

Spedding also, in giving some of the probabilities of Bacon's authorship of another poem of about a dozen lines, shows how far his mind is from the thought of Bacon as Shakespeare. He writes: "It is to be found in a volume of manuscript collections, but the hand is that of a copyist and tells us only that somebody has said or thought that the verses were by Bacon, a fact, however, which is worth rather more in this case than in many others, inasmuch as (verses not being in Bacon's line) a man merely guessing at the author is not likely to have thought of him. The internal evidence tells for little either way. They are such lines as might well have been written by Bacon or by a hundred other people."

His biographer, Abbot, says of these verses: "A true poet even of a low order could hardly betray the cramping influence of rhyme and metre * * * I cannot help coming to the conclusion that, although Bacon might have written better verse on some subject of his own choosing, the chances are that not even his best would have been very good."

I have copied what Bacon's historians say of his half dozen attempts at versification, because I wish to draw attention to the fact that the men who had such abundant opportunity to discover the nature of his life's work, speak of his few experiments in rhyme at the age of sixty—upwards—as a new form of mental activity. These men had made it the business of many years to learn everything concerning Bacon's life. They had searched every place and studied every piece of writing to discover and preserve any and everything, that could throw light upon his character and genius, and yet there is no hint of a suspicion that any rumour or report had ever reached them that he might be Shakespeare in disguise. **If they overlooked anything that could establish Bacon's right to Shakespeare's genius, then what they missed was infinitely more than what they found.**

It is a singular feature in this discussion that Bacon's biographers, who had access to his manuscripts, memorandums, letters, and the private recesses of his library, are not among those who connect him with Shakespeare. This is because the claim is not made upon evidence, but is simply a belief in Bacon founded upon a disbelief in Shakespeare. Bacon's biographers do not share this belief or disbelief. Mr. Devey, for instance, says, "In casting the horoscope of the future, or tracing, with certain hand, the progress of civilization, who shall account for the appearance of such men as Dante and Shakespeare, who have created a new language; of Cromwell and Luther, who have revolutionized empires; of Newton and Archimedes, who have introduced a new element into science?"

It is no obstacle to the belief of Bacon's friends, that the plays are the work of an average lifetime, that they were put upon the stage by Shakespeare, and that Bacon's biographers (and his brother to whom his manuscripts were bequeathed) found no scrap or hint of an incident to indicate or betray the accomplishment of such an immense work, and involving the agency of at least one other person.

When Bacon wrote the psalms, the plays of Shakespeare had been in existence many years, some at least thirty, none less than twelve; the sonnets thirty years, Lucrece nearly as long. To believe Bacon the author of the plays is therefore to suppose, not that he was an unskilled versifier when he wrote the psalms, but that the author of these awkward rhymes, was the ripe and unequalled poet who had already given Shakespeare's works to the world.

I have said, the plays had been in existence many years, but they existed in such an uncared-for shape that the attention of some one capable of appreciating their worth, and putting them in their original form, would doubtless have given them to us more complete and beautiful in many parts than we have them. As Bacon did nothing towards their preservation or publication (in such strong contrast with his solicitude for *his* writings), his indifference about them, or ignorance of them, cannot be reconciled with any claim to their authorship, and it seems as though his friends were willing to commit him to any absurdity, particularly those who picture him concocting a scheme to insure himself the fame in the future of having written the plays, while quite unconcerned what becomes of them in the present; especially as he had so little faith in the survival of the language in which the plays were written, that he had taken the precaution to put *his* works into a dead tongue to insure their perpetuity.

It should be very disheartening to any one looking for similarities between Shakespeare and Bacon, to compare the 104th Psalm with Bacon's rhyming version of it, as an instance:

104TH PSALM.

" 14. He causeth the grass to grow for the cattle, and the herb for the service of man: that he may bring forth food out of the earth;

" 15. And wine that maketh glad the heart of man, and oil to make his face to shine, and bread which strengtheneth man's heart."

Bacon's rendition reads:

"Causing the earth put forth the grass for beasts,
And garden herbs, served at the greatest feasts,
And bread that is all viands firmament,
And gives a firm and solid nourishment,
And wine, man's spirits for to recreate,
And oil, his face for to exhilarate."

This would pass for a travesty. The material sense even, is not well preserved, whilst every particle of sublimity, spirituality, and poetic beauty of diction in the original, is eradicated and destroyed. The thing of first importance to the Baconite theory is to prove that Bacon never wrote these lines. While they exist as his production, they must be accepted as the gauge of his ability, and that is fatal to the claim that is made for him. They are witnesses that must be silenced. They could not be inserted in any Shakespeare piece and escape detection by a school boy. They compare unfavorably with anything in print of that age. They who think that Shakespeare needed Bacon's learning to enable him to write the plays, may judge from this versification how much Bacon's learning contributed to his poetry.

The use of the words "do" and "for to" may be intended as very stately and formal, and at that time *perhaps* may not have been considered so inelegant as now; but the repetition, line after line, of such unvaried terms exposes a dearth of fancy, imagination and taste, and is most tiresome and unpleasing. In the selections from a hundred different poets and ballad writers which I have seen collected in one volume, from 1400 to 1626, the year of Bacon's death, there is not anything that is not infinitely superior to Bacon's verses, which I think have never received the compliment of being printed in any collection of poems, and, so far as I know, have never appeared outside of his own works, or in any book or article on this subject, and I doubt if many people know they exist. His verses prove not only that he was not a poet, but that he had not a conception of poetic grace and sentiment, sufficient to teach him how weak and trashy his attempt was. Instead of hiding or burning this production *he published it;* an act upon which Spedding comments in this wise: "Considering how little he had cared to publish during the first sixty years of his life, and how many things of weightier character and more careful workmanship he had then by him in his cabinet, it was somewhat remarkable."

Every reader will endorse Mr. Spedding's opinion, but this singular act is one of the strongest evidences against Bacon's authorship of the plays; quite as convincing as the wretchedness of his poetry; for it shows his ardent ambition to pose before the world in the new *rôle* of poet. With this desire so rampant, his neglect to assume the title to Shakespeare, had he owned it, would have been more remarkable than the publication of his verses.

It is impossible to imagine the author and publisher of such lines rising to the genius of the plays, or the author of the plays falling to the level of such verse.

The theory of the Baconites is that Bacon concealed his authorship of the plays because such writing was held in low esteem and might, if known, have been an obstacle to his advancement at court. In the course of these pages I shall endeavour to show this assumption to be untrue, but supposing that it were true; and granting him Shakespeare's genius, why should he confine himself to writing plays? It is reasonable to expect that of Shakespeare—although he did not confine himself to it—for he was an actor and the stage was his profession and livelihood, but Bacon had no such interest and had no association with the theatrical people, except with Ben Jonson, in Latin study. If a prejudice existed against play writing there was certainly none against such poems as

Spencer, Sydney, Raleigh, and many others wrote, or against Shakespeare's sonnets. If Bacon wrote the sonnets why should he disown them? If Shakespeare wrote the sonnets, why could he not have written the plays?

The theory of Bacon's champions supposes that he never wrote the things which he might safely acknowledge, but that he schemed and laboured to produce such works as would imperil his reputation and position. It cannot be conceived that he would have felt no pride in his art; that he would not have been recognized as were other poets of his time; or that he would not have contributed largely to the verse of that age had he possessed such talent, and it cannot be accepted that he would have devoted such genius and labour to a calling that he considered "corrupt and disreputable," and which could bring him little, if any, profit, but which, if his friend's views are correct, might do him much mischief. It is frequently urged by the friends of Shakespeare that he could not have secured and maintained such reputation, the respect and love of his fellows, and the constant support of his patrons if he had been incapable of writing the plays that he produced. It is fully as pertinent to point out that Bacon could not have concealed such talent from the wits and critics of the age had he possessed it. Neither could he have suppressed all exhibition of it in his outward life, and every trace of it, in his known works. His sphere of activity, the nature of his ambition, and his companionships appear to have been as far removed from the tastes and sympathies of the other famous poets of his day, as from Shakespeare. He was over thirty years of age when Shakespeare's first plays appeared, and he lived fifteen years after Shakespeare retired from the stage, yet no Shakespeare plays were produced either before or after these dates. If Shakespeare had been simply Bacon's mask his absence would have necessitated merely a substitute—Ben Jonson, for instance, who continued in the profession all his life, twenty-one years after Shakespeare died and eleven years after the death of Bacon. Why did Bacon's muse expire when Shakespeare left the stage?

It is given as an explanation of *the fact that the plays appeared only during Shakespeare's twenty years' connection with the theatre*, that after that time Bacon became Attorney-General to James I., and was too much engaged in political duties to allow himself time for literary work: this will not account for his writing no poetry whatever except the psalms —if they may be called poetry—during forty-six years of his life, and it is especially weak from the fact that he did perform much literary work after that period; the greater part of his works were published after Shakespeare's death. Bacon was never busier than at the time of the Essex trials, 1601, when the production of Shakespeare's plays did not flag in the least, and for twenty years Bacon's time was as fully absorbed in the pursuit of office, as would have been possible in the performance of the duties after attainment.

If there is any truth in his biographers' accounts of his financial straits and his twenty years of begging and scheming for appointment, his final success with King James gave him the leisure and comparative respite from his creditors needed for reflective work, but time, and opportunity, according to the Baconite theory, was not of much consequence to Bacon in writing these plays. All his known works were revised, rewritten, reissued, translated into a dead language, carefully kept in a cabinet until his death and provided for in his will. We are to suppose that the plays were his little sins against the Puritanical prejudice of the age, tossed off by stealth at the rate of two a year for some twenty years, unsuspected by even his secretary and unbetrayed by a scrap of paper, the scratch of a pen, or a blotch of ink. The people who cannot explain how, when, or where their idol wrote the plays, should find some more likely reason than a want of time, to account for his entire lack of poetic impulse during two-thirds of his lifetime, and during all the time that Shakespeare was not present to shield him from the disgrace of possessing poetic and dramatic genius.

CHAPTER II.

Repugnance to the Baconites' claim—Queen Elizabeth's estimate of Bacon—His doubt of the permanency of the English language—His quotations—His opinion of stage acting—His Essay on Masques and Triumphs—Ben Jonson's description of Shakespeare's strolling company.

AMONG the lovers of Shakespeare there is a repugnance to the thought of attributing his authorship to Bacon that would not be felt to nearly the same degree if the claim were made for Marlowe, Marston, Dekker, and a number of others. These men were Shakespeare's friends; the stage was their livelihood; their hearts were in this art; they loved and honoured their profession, and had dramatic talent of a high order.

The heart warms to them for their comradeship with Shakespeare, and willingly accords them some of his glory, but Bacon's inferiority in everything that constitutes Shakespeare's charm, his expressed contempt for the stage, and the mean motive upon which his claim to

Shakespeare's works is based—that from fear or shame he disowned them—stir up a feeling of protest as though the plays themselves were threatened with some loss or irreparable injury.

The lovers of the plays demand that they shall have an honest origin and a manly author, and will not believe that they could have been written in fear and shame, sneaked out of a back door and imposed upon the wittiest and brightest people of that age, under circumstances that would disgrace all concerned. Considering the undisputed place that is given them, it is natural that any question of their authorship should awaken a deep interest; but it is singular that any one should be willing to dethrone the man who positively put them on the stage, and whose claim to them was absolutely unquestioned during his lifetime and for more than two centuries after his death, without, at least, a most searching test of the right of the new claimant. It is singular also that people should so passively echo the refrain of the doubters as to the college-bred requirements of their author. The most beautiful parts in Shakespeare are in the simplest language, and there is nothing in the story of the plays that the genius that produced the verse could not have learned from reading.

The one essential that learning and study could not supply was the mind and genius of Shakespeare. The intellectual feature of the subject is, however, not the only one to be considered; the character, tastes, and employments of the two men enter almost as deeply into the possibility of authorship as does the question of learning and scholarly ability, and in these respects no two men were ever more unlike. The "precepts" for Laertes are fully observed in Shakespeare's life, but violated in every phase of Bacon's history:

>"To thine own self be true,
>And it must follow, as the night the day,
>Thou canst not then be false to any man."

It may be urged that Bacon's writings are in accord with the philosophy of the plays, even if his character was not, and therefore that his career cannot be cited against him as their author. It is my conviction that this is not true, and that his writings plainly teach the methods by which he lived; that his rules of life, his ambition, tastes, principles and prejudices were totally antagonistic to the spirit of the plays, not artistically alone, but in all the truth that they affirm and all the wrong that they expose. This I shall hereafter endeavour to demonstrate by his own expressions.

It is impossible to doubt Shakespeare's sincerity. Each one unconsciously and irresistibly forms an idea of an author, justifying or rejecting what he conveys to the imagination, and thus to the lovers of Shakespeare, the incomparable poet is a lovable man, full of nobility and manhood, and cannot be a corrupt judge and servile politician.

"Gentle, never schooled and yet learned, full of noble device, of all sorts enchantingly beloved."

It is singular that Bacon's learning should give him any claim to dramatic genius or power. He was a great student, and a ready, voluble lawyer. He was well read in everything extant at the time, and had above everything else a marvellous memory, but limited originality, whilst his extreme love for the prosaic studies of law and physics diminishes the probability of any poetic temperament, even were it left to conjecture to determine this point, but he has not failed to express his superiority to fiction and to works of the imagination.

If I have ventured very far in doubting his more than ordinary originality, I have very distinguished authority of his own time to sustain my disbelief; one indeed who knew him intimately; one to whom he gave a new year's gift, 1599-1600, described as follows: "By Mr. Frauncis Bacon, one pettycote of white satten, embrothered all over like feathers and billets, with three brode borders, faire embrothered with snakes and frutage:" none other than Queen Elizabeth herself, who said of him, "Bacon hath great wit and learning, but in law he showeth to the uttermost of his knowledge, and is not deep."

It is reasonable to suppose that if Bacon had written the plays they would have been translated into Latin as his published works were. I think there is nothing over his signature, except his letters, that has not, at least, a Latin title. While he was so unappreciative of the English language, and held it so cheaply that he would not entrust his writings to it, Shakespeare was discovering and creating a depth of power, expression, feeling and beauty in it, that alone, would make it immortal. It is a very strong side-light upon the improbability of Bacon's hand in these writings, that they are the masterpieces of a language that he valued so lightly. To him a dead tongue was more than the living language in which the plays were written.

Another feature that is very prominent in Bacon's writings and which is also in striking contrast with Shakespeare, is his monumental habit of quotation, allusion, illustration and reference to other writings, occasions and incidents. It is boundless. It gives evidence of most extensive reading and phenomenal memory. He had a habit of jotting down whatever caught his attention, both in his reading and in occurrences. He could not, however, have used notes simply, with such facility. He must have had a memory, quick and ready, that could be always depended upon. His writings unprofessional are brimful of such instances. Every page and almost every paragraph contains them. It is the scaffolding upon which he supports all his speculative theories, and is, often, by far the most interesting and substantial part of the structure. His works are so full of this kind of padding, borrowed from every conceivable source, that they would not hold together without it. They would be "very rags." This habit of illustration by analogy drawn from such a vast range of subjects, which embellished his pages, and at the same time displayed his learning, was not only a necessity to him, but it was his undisguised pride. He says, in Advancement of Learning, "The way of delivery by aphorisms has numerous advantages over the methodical. First, it gives us a proof of the author's abilities, and shows whether he hath entered deep into his subject or not." One who has a happy faculty of using the thoughts of others makes them half his own. Bacon fully appreciated that. The foreign matter that he crammed into his Essays was the pith of them. In them he never stood alone. He used everything he could capture to extend his articles even if he had to strain the life and shape out of it as his witness. He certainly possessed this faculty to an uncommon extent, and it was a valuable help to him, but it is the very opposite of originality. Although he used so much that was not his own and may have made it serve his purpose then, it does not bear criticism now. His nature was so material that he could scarcely comprehend the spiritual and moral in any true sense, and much that he quoted he distorted into meanings contrary to its original intention.

Yet this habitual citing of instances to support his theories and gain his ends exhibited him at his best and gave him great power and renown.

I have emphasized this habit of straining after supports to show how different it is from Shakespeare. Mr. Fred. Gard Fleay, in his Life of Shakespeare, page 75, says, " For Marlowe he had a sincere regard ; from his poem of Hero and Leander, *Shakespeare makes the only direct quotation to be found in his plays ;* on his (Marlowe's) historical plays Shakespeare, after his friend's decease, bestowed in addition, revision and completion, a greater amount of minute work than on his own."

If I were candidly trying to convince myself that Bacon wrote the plays, I should feel it essential to my belief that some probable reason should be found to explain this dissimilarity, which is so distinct and which exposes such measureless inequality in the writings. It is only necessary to read Bacon, especially his speculative works, to see that it does exist, not simply to some degree, but absolutely. In Bacon the quotations are the prominent feature which immediately catch the attention. I have found as many as fourteen on one page. In Shakespeare we feel that such an instance could hardly fail to disturb the harmony and mar the purity of the perfect work. Shakespeare could only have borrowed from those poorer than himself.

Such an unlikeness in the writings of the same author, in this particular alone, is hardly possible even with the most studied care and intention, but conceding that possibility, the motive is still wanting. The least that such an argument could assume would be that Bacon had bestowed great care upon the plays, and had felt a greater fondness for them than for his other works. Both of these assumptions are contradicted by his own testimony and by all the facts. He never claimed the plays; though they would have been the greatest aid to his ambition, he did nothing toward preserving and publishing them, and he wrote most contemptuously of the stage.

The contrast between them in this respect

is not explainable upon any supposition that one brain produced Shakespeare's plays and Bacon's works. It is not possible that Bacon could have completely dropped the habit which is so conspicuous in all his writings, had he wished to, and it is equally unreasonable to suppose a desire on his part to avoid an art in which he excelled, and of which he was evidently very vain. I do not think he could have written anything on ethics without such prompting and suggestion. It is not possible that Bacon could have been as superior to himself as Shakespeare is superior to Bacon's known works: and it is not possible that Bacon could have had the genius and power to write the Shakespeare plays, and have been considered "not deep" by a woman of Queen Elizabeth's penetration. She also made great pretension to learning; wrote and translated books, and made ready replies in Greek and Latin.

Bacon's method of showing if one "hath entered deep into his subject" accords precisely with the Queen's pithy estimate of his powers. His method was to read exhaustively and quote voluminously, and she evidently meant that in law he found a field in which he could exercise and display his attainments, but "he was not deep," *i.e.*, original.

Bacon was in every act, sentiment, and expression antagonistic to Shakespeare's tastes and calling. He has furnished evidence at every point that he was not the author of the plays. He had no love for the theatre, but regarded it with great disfavour and wrote most disparagingly of it. In one place he says, "Though the thing itself be disreputable in the profession of it, yet it is excellent as a discipline, we mean the action of the theatre." Again, "Dramatic poetry which has the theatre for its world, would be of excellent use if it were sound; for the discipline and corruption of the theatre is of very great consequence. Now, of this corruption we have enough. Modern play acting is but a toy except when it is too biting and satirical, but the ancients used it as a means of educating men's minds to virtue; and certain it is, though a great secret in nature, that men's minds in company are more open to affections and impressions than when alone."

Again, he gives his pedantic estimate of its proper purpose and use in language so far removed from any sign of interest in or enjoyment of it, that this paragraph alone should invalidate any claim to dramatic sense, feeling, or conception. He writes, "I mean stage playing; an act which strengthens the memory, regulates the tone and effect of the voice and pronunciation, teaches a decent carriage of the countenance and gesture, gives not a little assurance, and accustoms young men to bear being looked at."

That is Bacon's summing up of the utility of the drama, of the stage, and of the player's action. It was a "thing" and disreputable as a profession. Modern theatres were a corruption of which they had enough, and acting in Shakespeare's time was "a toy," except when it became too much of a satire.

The extracts given are not from any article written upon the subject of the stage, he never wrote any such; they are simply expressions that crop out in regard to it among his speculative rambles. The wide range of his observations justifies a belief that he did not intend to leave posterity ignorant of his views upon any subject, and his notice of the stage is general and passing, without special design.

He indicates no fixed interest, and the chief stress is laid upon its degeneracy, corruption, and general worthlessness.

The first tragedy written in the English language was performed during Queen Elizabeth's reign. Up to a short time previous to this, only Scriptural plays had been given. Bacon evidently referred to that kind of stage acting as the sound use to which the ancients had devoted the stage. He wanted it to preach a sermon; and as it did not do that, the only good that he could find in it was a school of elocution. It strengthened the memory—of course committing the *rôles* would catch his matter-of-fact attention—and he could appreciate the benefit to the memory.

At that time Shakespeare's plays were not only new, but it was a new epoch for the stage. Bacon's Ancients had departed, and in their place appeared the genius, poetry and humour of living men to "hold the mirror up to nature." One can only try to imagine the wonder, surprise and joy of the audiences. Even now when we have seen and read the plays until we know them almost as well as the actors, they still possess us to the extent that disillusion is never welcome. Then what a niggard comprehension of the drama must a man have had who after seeing Shakespeare's plays could write only that "the thing," "play acting, strengthens the memory, accustoms young men to bear being looked at," is corrupt and not sound as it was with the ancients.

It is of no consequence what Bacon's opinion of the stage was, except as to the bearing it has upon the subject of the authorship. At that time, when Shakespeare's plays were coming upon the stage, and their fame was such that both his name and his works were pirated upon, Bacon had no more appreciation of their incomparable beauty or sense of their marvellous dramatic merit than a sneer at the stage, which he dismissed with a few paragraphs of contemptuous drivel.

If he had ever written for the stage, he would not have bestowed so little attention upon it in his works, and certainly would not have stigmatized it as corrupt; neither would he have preferred the ancient stage if his own plays were being acted on the modern. If he had written plays, they would have been plays of the character he described, which the ancients used to perform. The kind of a play that Bacon might have written, and which would not have been a "toy" or "too biting," and which would have been "sound," is set forth in his New Atlantis.

It would have been inconsistent with human nature for him to lament the corruption of the stage if the productions of his own pen were then its chief attractions. There is nowhere an indication of the possibility of his expressing condemnation of anything that emanated from Francis of Verulam, stigmatizing it as "a toy," or as too biting and satirical. If he had produced the Shakespeare plays he would have spoken of them as seen from the stage; he would not have been so unappreciative of their innate power as to attribute their effect simply to "the great secret in nature" that people are more affected in a body than singly. He was not the man to belittle his own work, and especially if he had any interest in its success. If he had remained entirely silent about the stage, his admirers might have discovered that to be a part of the scheme of concealment, as though he had avoided the subject intentionally, but the apparently careless manner in which he mentions the subject and occasionally recurs to it, then so quickly disposes of it with such commonplace, superficial comments—all in perfect keeping with his grave and lofty "Francis of Verulam thought thus"—indicates that the subject did not interest him. One cannot imagine the writer of such plays indifferent about their appearance upon the stage, and it is not possible that a man could feel any interest in the stage and write of it as Bacon did.

The test of a play is its presentation on the stage. This is the thought to which the writer addresses himself. He has as defined an idea of all the details of the stage setting, as about the plot and the sentiment. His characters are to him realities, who must play their parts as he conceives them, and therefore his business is not finished with his manuscript. There is, perhaps, nothing that expresses this as forcibly as a play within a play, as Hamlet, where he instructs the actors how they shall speak and what faults they shall avoid, and the "Critic," in which the author is present at the rehearsals. That is the solicitude for the effect of the play. It is the fear that it may be marred in the acting and setting. Aside from the desire to avoid faults common to the stage, an author has a taste and fancy about his work, which he may fear the text does not fully convey.

This is the unwritten part of the play which must be finished on the stage. It is the breathing of active life into the lines, vital to the art and purpose of the dramatist. It is, perhaps, largely owing to an appreciation of this fact that the Baconians find no converts among theatrical people. It is pleasant to imagine, from the history of the plays and of the man who wrote them, that they were written in the theatre and created on the stage; one may well wonder with what sort of feeling the advocates of the Bacon theory regard productions which they believe to have been conceived in shame, born amidst politics and law books, and abandoned by their creator.

Bacon's expressions in regard to the stage taken in their most favourable light would denote a contemptuous unconcern. My belief is that he would have been an active enemy to the stage if the court had not protected it, and I shall show by his essay on Masques and

Triumphs that he only tolerated such "toys" because "princes will have them."

There was nothing in the theatre or in amusements that appealed to his nature. To him the theatre was frivolous. He was engaged in realities. That there could be instruction in anything but a discourse or essay, and particularly in anything as disreputable as the theatre, in his time, he probably never suspected.

If, however, the actors could have personated such characters as he has created in the New Atlantis, where there is "no touch of love," and the women are not permitted to speak, with dialogues full of flattery of kings and princes, interspersed with homilies upon artificial virtue and soliloquies of crafty wisdom, then Bacon's plays might have been presented; **but it would have been the death, and not the birth, of the drama.**

In Bacon's time there was a kind of dramatic performance, called Masques, which was quite popular at court. The ladies and gentlemen of the court took part, and persons were hired to perform the inferior *rôles*. It is said that Ben Jonson and the leading dramatists wrote for them, but *Shakespeare did not.* Bacon wrote an essay upon these performances, which is similar to what I have quoted from his other writings. Indeed, I have never found an expression in his writings at variance with these opinions in regard to the theatre. Even in his Novum Organum he has created a department which he calls "idols of the theatre." They have no reference to the stage, but the name of the theatre is applied to them as condemnatory. As he is writing of science his inborn repugnance to the stage suggests to him the fitness of the term theatre to describe that which is to him impure and trifling. He says, " The idols of the theatre are not innate, nor do they introduce themselves secretly into the understanding, but they are manifestly instilled and cherished by fictions of theories and depraved rules of demonstration." Again he says, "There are idols which have crept into men's minds from the various dogmas of peculiar systems of philosophy, and also from the perverted rules of demonstration, and these we denominate idols of the theatre ; for we regard all the systems of philosophy hitherto received or imagined as so many plays brought out and performed, creating fictitious and theatrical worlds."

If Bacon had written plays these Masques would have furnished him an excellent opportunity to place one of his productions before the court, where it would not have been professional or disreputable, and where it would not have blighted his career or stabbed his reputation. Milton's Comus was such a production. He did not entitle it Comus, but simply "A Masque," and it was presented at Ludlow Castle in 1634 before the Earl of Bridgewater, President of Wales. Milton was eighteen years old at the time of Bacon's death. His political career shows that his dramatic genius was no obstacle to his advancement, and consequently there was no political obstacle to Bacon's appearing as a dramatic poet at these court masques.

In fact, dramatic writing would have lost him no esteem at court. It was not *writing*, but *acting*, that was disreputable; the court was friendly to the theatrical companies, interposed to protect them, and contributed to their support on some occasions. I shall show this to have been conspicuously true. The people who opposed the theatre were not the party in power, to whom Bacon looked for favours. It is probable that Bacon's prospects would have been improved rather than injured if he had been known as the author of the plays. Certainly Queen Elizabeth would have rated his mental gifts more highly. Ben Jonson was a writer and something of an actor, and was very popular among the nobility. He was a guest at Bacon's celebration of his sixtieth anniversary and wrote some lines relative to the occasion. There is no evidence whatever to show that *writing* the plays would have caused any feeling, either in Queen Elizabeth or King James, adverse to Bacon's political ambition. They were both patrons of the stage and particularly appreciative of Shakespeare's plays, as the number of performances at Christmas festivities verifies.

If he had been a writer of plays, it is singular that he should not write a masque, particularly as he attended at least one and wrote an essay on it.

He took part in the production of one of these shows in 1587, when he was twenty-eight years of age—about the time Shakespeare went to London. This afforded a fine opportunity for displaying his genius to the queen, for whose favour and notice he was always a suppliant, but the record shows, that notwithstanding so convenient a temptation, the legend was the work of Hughes, and the only part Bacon took was in the spectacular "dumb show and noise." He also figures in connection with a similar diversion, presented before King James, in 1612, when he was solicitor-general, and feverishly importunate for the king's gracious consideration, but he also let pass this "golden chance" to discard the mask and appear as the man.

If Shakespeare had been his mask he certainly would have been conspicuous on such an occasion; instead of that, Shakespeare does not write for, or take any part in that kind of hippodrome performance, but Bacon writes a kind of critique upon it, noticing only the grosser parts.

"OF MASQUES AND TRIUMPHS."

"These things are but toys to come amongst such serious observations; but yet, since princes will have such things, it is better they should be graced with elegancy than daubed with cost. Dancing to song is a thing of great state and pleasure. I understand it that the song be in quire placed aloft and accompanied with some broken music, and the ditty fitted to the device. Acting in song, especially in dialogues, hath an extreme good grace; I say acting, not dancing (for that is a mean and vulgar thing); and the voices of the dialogue would be strong and manly (a base and a tenor; no treble), and the ditty high and tragical, not nice and dainty. Several quires placed one over against another and taking the voice by catches, anthem-wise, give great pleasure. Turning dances into figure is a childish curiosity; and generally, let it be noted that those things which I here set down are such as do naturally take the sense, and not respect petty wonderments. It is true, the alterations of the scenes, so it be quietly and without noise, are things of great beauty and pleasure, for they feed and relieve the eye before it be full of the same object. Let the scenes abound with light, specially coloured and varied; and let the masquers or any other that are to come down from the scene have some motions upon the scene itself before their coming down; for it draws the eye strangely, and makes it with great pleasure to desire to see that, it cannot perfectly discern. Let the songs be loud and cheerful, and not chirpings or pulings; let the music likewise be sharp and loud, and well placed. The colours that show best by candlelight are white, carnation and a kind of sea-water green ; and ouches or spangs, as they are of no great cost, so they are of most glory. As for rich embroidery, it is lost and not discerned. Let the suits of the masquers be graceful, and such as become the person when the visors are off; not after examples of known attires; Turks, soldiers, mariners, and the like. Let anti-masques not be long; they have been commonly of fools, satyrs, babboons, wild men, antics, beasts, sprites, witches, Ethiopes, pigmies, turquets, nymphs, rustics, Cupids, statues moving, and the like. As for angels, it is not comical enough to put them in anti-masques; and anything that is hideous, as devils, giants, is, on the other side, as unfit; but chiefly, let the music of them be recreative, and with some strange changes. Some sweet odours suddenly coming forth, without any drops falling, are, in such a company as there is steam and heat, things of great pleasure and refreshment. Double masques, one of men, another of ladies, addeth state and variety; but all is nothing, except the room be kept clean and neat. For jousts and turneys, and barriers, the glories of them are chiefly in the chariots; wherein the challengers make their entry, especially if they be drawn with strange beasts. But enough of these toys."

That is as near a dramatic critique as anything to be found in Bacon's writings. It sounds as if he were talking of something uninteresting to him, and that he in reality knew little of. It is impossible to imagine the writer of that article plotting with Shakespeare for aid in concealing his brilliancy and to save him from the unhappy results of an exposure of his dramatic ability. Yet this is the whole theory upon which the Baconian claim is grounded.

This essay is faithful to his habitual temper. He commences by calling the Masques "toys" and finishes with the same epithet. It begins with an apology and ends with a shrug. He murmurs at the necessity of interrupting such serious observations as his studies, but yields because "princes will have such things." He shows that he has no knowledge of what he is saying, by flatly contradicting himself at the start, as, "dancing to song is a thing of great state and pleasure," and immediately afterwards, "it is a mean and vulgar thing." How a "stately" dance can be a great pleasure I do not know, but that is the adjective that describes everything that Bacon approves. There is no thought or mention of sentiment. He sees it only as a flashy spectacle and commends the "dumb show and noise," traversing Shakespeare's advice to the players: "Anything so overdone is from the purpose of playing"; every material part is noticed. The story, the dialogue, the imaginative, is not.

The things which catch his attention are the "strong and manly voice," the loud and tragical ditty, the sharp, loud music, scenery, light and costumes. The figures of the dance ruffle his stately muse: they are but "childish curiosity." He will not have a ditty that is "nice and dainty." He suggests the infusion of perfumes, for obvious reasons—does not want the company sprinkled, however—and thinks it all amounts to nothing unless the room be clean and neat.

Contrast his loud and pompous discourse with

"*Oberon*.—Through the house with glimmering light,
By the dead and drowsy fire;
Every elf and fairy sprite
Hop as light as bird from brier,
And this ditty, after me,
Sing and dance it trippingly."

Comment cannot heighten the contrast between the light, elfish and fairy grace of the Midsummer Night's Dream and this lumpish critique upon Masques and Triumphs. Everything in Bacon suggests its opposite in Shakespeare, and not its counterpart. Even the mention of the neat, clean room as essential to the success of the masque recalls a sentence from Ben Jonson, which gives a speaking picture of a travelling detachment of Shakespeare's company in contrast with the orderly requisites indispensable to Bacon's enjoyment (?) of theatricals.

This sentence is quoted in Fleay's Life of Shakespeare. Shakespeare's company was journeying through the country, and Jonson published a dialogue in the Poetaster, in which he sought to make it appear that their necessity to travel was due to the inefficiency of their play writers, and (referring to Shakespeare's company) he puts this speech in the dialogue : "If thou wilt employ Marston, who pens high lofty, in a new stalking strain, thou shalt not need to travel with thy pumps full of gravel after a blind jade, and a hamper and stalk upon boards and barrel heads, to an old cracked trumpet."

Ben Jonson was connected with a rival theatre. The picture which he draws of Shakespeare's company may be somewhat exaggerated, but there is abundant other evidence of the same nature to show that the theatrical profession offered no temptation to Bacon to embark in it with a view to money making. It describes a condition in every respect totally uncongenial to him, and heightens the improbability of a pecuniary object to him, in play writing.

Jonson's fling at Shakespeare, as the writer for his company, not only reveals the precarious fortunes of the actors, but also exposes the circumstances under which the plays were performed, in contrast with the neat and orderly requirements which Bacon laid so much stress upon. It is a very graphic picture of a strolling company. It suggests scanty receipts, a sorry equipment, cold meats, a thin orchestra, the roughest improvisation of a stage, and any chance building for a theatre or shelter, but it is safe to assume that the rustics who filled the barns where the supposed "blind jade" was also quartered, had a treat that was not disturbed by the perfumes or want of perfumes, and the audience that would flock to-day to see the player who "stalked" upon the stage with "barrel head" underpinnings would not be as critical about the surroundings as Bacon was. These extracts defining Bacon's attitude towards the stage are as positive as he could make them. They express both indifference and aversion. They are his carefully-prepared thoughts: not what his historians say of him simply, but what he has written and scattered all through his works, and translated into classic language that it may endure to his renown.

The slighting manner in which he treats the subject is simply in harmony with his estimate of the place the stage merited in comparison with the questions worthy of his thought. Even as a pastime for the court, he felt it a compromise with his dignity to suspend his "serious observations" to notice it. In this essay he does not leave it to be inferred that he has a taste for the lighter and finer parts of the masques, but calls attention that he has noticed the things which "do naturally take the sense and not respect petty wonderments."

CHAPTER III.

The stage as a symbol—Shakespeare—Bacon—Bacon's notes on conversation—Hamlet's advice to the players—Bacon's apparatus of rhetoric—The Epitaph—Bacon's Tomb—The Cipher—The proclivities of Shakespeare and Bacon—Bacon as an Inquisitor—The quality of mercy—Bacon as a friend—Bacon's grants of patents to monopolies—Macaulay's estimate of Bacon's character—His servility to Buckingham—His pamphlet in favour of religious war—His falsification of history—Fairness of authorities quoted.

IN contrast with Bacon's opinion of the superficial use and influence of the stage, the plays contain parts so pointedly adverse to his expressions as to suggest the idea that they might be written in reply, or in its defence against such attacks. Bacon says modern play acting is a "toy," is "corrupt" and "unsound." Shakespeare: "Playing, whose end both at the first, and now, was, and is, to hold as 'twere, the mirror up to nature; to show virtue her own feature, scorn her own image, and the very age and body of the time his form and pressure."

The use of the stage as a symbol, as it frequently occurs in Shakespeare, suggests the work of an actor and one whose mind dwells strongly upon his profession. The "seven ages" could never have been the thought of a man who uses the stage as an illustration of that which is depraved and false. Bacon, in his Aphorisms, describes "perverted rules of demonstration as so many plays brought out and performed, creating fictitious and theatrical worlds."

To Bacon the stage was a prompt and suitable illustration of what was false, fictitious and unreal. In Shakespeare's mind it embraced "all the world," and proclaimed the nobility of his art.

> " Life is a walking shadow, a poor player
> That struts and frets his hour upon the stage,
> And then is heard no more. It is a tale,
> Told by an idiot, full of sound and fury
> Signifying nothing."

> " This wide and universal theatre
> Presents more woeful pageants than the scene
> Wherein we act in."

> " All the world's a stage,
> And all the men and women merely players :
> They have their exits and their entrances ;
> And one man in his time plays many parts,
> His acts being seven ages. At first the infant,
> Mewling and puking in the nurse's arms.
> And then the whining school-boy with his satchel
> And shining morning face, creeping like snail

Unwillingly to school. And then the lover,
Sighing like furnace, with a woeful ballad
Made to his mistress' eyebrow. Then a soldier
Full of strange oaths and bearded like the pard,
Jealous in honor, sudden and quick in quarrel,
Seeking the bubble reputation
Even in the cannon's mouth. And then the justice
In fair round belly with good capon lined,
With eyes severe and beard of formal cut,
Full of wise saws and modern instances ;
And so he plays his part. The sixth age shifts
Into the lean and slippered pantaloon,
With spectacles on nose and pouch on side,
His youthful hose well saved, a world too wide
For his shrunk shank ; and his big manly voice,
Turning again towards childish treble, pipes
And whistles in his sound. Last scene of all,
That ends this strange, eventful history,
Is second childishness and mere oblivion,
Sans teeth, sans eyes, sans taste, sans everything."

These lines evince a familiarity with the stage and a fondness for it that cannot be supposed of Bacon. His regrets were for its *past*. Shakespeare's belief was in its *future*. One who would cavil at the degeneracy of the stage would hardly choose it as a symbol of life and "its strange, eventful history," or of all that the world contained for him :—

"I hold the world but as the world, Gratiano :
A stage where every man must play a part,
And mine a sad one."

Bacon was as shortsighted a seer of the future of the stage and its influence, as of the vitality and power of the English language. He chose a tongue that was passing from life to "enshrine" his thoughts that they should not perish, and was so wide of the mark that they need to be translated, to be read by his countrymen. While supposing that he was going forward he was in reality faced toward the past, and he chose the stage as a figure to represent the systems of philosophy which he held in contempt and disowned.

The simple citation of his expressions wherever they touch upon subjects akin to Shakespeare's plays, is all the argument needed in denial of any propensity in his nature toward such diversion. He had the same disdain of fiction and works of the imagination as of the stage. He wrote no romance (always excepting the "New Atlantis"), humour, or fancy. The character of the writings of the two men is so unlike that it is difficult to find instances where they have treated precisely the same subject. Some examples may be found, however, approaching nearly enough to the same theme to afford a fair opportunity for comparison.

Bacon's "Short Notes on Civil Conversations," for instance, is addressed to the same purpose as Hamlet's advice to the players. If it does not compare closely it may stand as an example of Bacon's prose, which, we are frequently assured, is like Shakespeare's verse.

"SHORT NOTES ON CIVIL CONVERSATIONS.

"To deceive men's expectations generally (with cautel) argueth a staid mind and unexpected constancy, viz., in matters of fear, anger, sudden joy or grief, and all things which may effect or alter the mind in public or sudden accidents or such like.

"It is necessary to use a steadfast countenance, not waiving with action as in moving the head or hand too much, which showeth a fantastical light and fickle operation of the spirit and consequently like mind as gesture; only it is sufficient with leisure to use a modest action in either.

"In all kinds of speech, either pleasant, grave, severe or ordinary, it is convenient to speak leisurely and rather drawingly than hastily; because hasty speech confounds the memory and oftentimes (besides unseemliness) drives a man either to a non plus, or unseemly stammering, harping upon that which should follow; whereas, a slow speech confirmeth the memory, addeth a conceit of wisdom to the hearers besides a seemliness of speech and countenance.

"To desire in discourse to hold all argument is ridiculous, wanting true judgment, for in all things no man can be exquisite.

"To have commonplaces to discourse and to want variety is both tedious to the hearers and shows a shallowness of conceit, therefore it is good to vary and suit speeches with the present occasions, and to have a moderation in all speeches, especially in jesting, of religion, state, great persons, weighty and important business, poverty and anything that deserves pity.

"To use many circumstances ere you come to matter is wearisome; and to use none at all is but blunt.

"Bashfulness is a great hindrance to a man both in uttering his conceit and understanding what is propounded unto him wherefore it is good to press himself forwards with discretion both in speech and in company of the better sort."

"*Hamlet.*—Speak the speech, I pray you, as I pronounce it to you, trippingly on the tongue; but if you mouth it as many of your players do, I had as lief the town crier spoke my lines. Nor do not saw the air too much with your hands, thus, but use all gently; for in the very torrent, tempest, as I may say whirlwind of passion, you must acquire and beget a temperance that may give it smoothness. Oh, it offends me to the very soul to hear a robustious, periwig-pated fellow tear a passion to tatters, to very rags, to split the ears of the groundlings, who for the most part are capable of nothing but inexplicable dumb show and noise. I would have such a fellow whipped for o'erdoing Termagant. It out-herods Herod. Pray you avoid it.

"Be not too tame neither, but let your own discretion be your tutor; suit the action to the word, the word to the action, with this special observance that you o'erstep not the modesty of nature; for anything so overdone is from the purpose of playing, whose end, both at the first, and now, was, and is, to hold, as 'twere, the mirror up to nature; to show virtue her own feature, scorn her own image, and the very age and body of the time his form and pressure. Now this overdone, or come tardy off, though it make the unskilful laugh, cannot but make the judicious grieve ; the censure of the which one, must, in your allowance, o'erweigh a whole theatre of others. Oh, there be players, that I have seen play, and heard others praise, and that highly, not to speak it profanely, that neither having the accent of Christians nor the gait of Christian, pagan, nor man, have so strutted and bellowed, that I have thought some of nature's journeymen had made men, and not made them well, they imitated humanity so abominably."

Considering Bacon's extensive reading and familiarity with the literature of the day, which must have included very much upon the subject of speech and conversation, it is singular that he should have thought such a composition as his Short Notes of sufficient merit or value for publication.

As another example, compare an aphorism with Shakespeare's apostrophe to man :—

Bacon's Aphorism No. 1.—"Man as the minister and interpreter of nature does and understands as much as his observation on the order of nature, either with regard to things or the mind permit him, and neither knows nor is capable of more."

"*Hamlet.*—What a piece of work is man, how noble in reason, how infinite in faculty, in form and moving, how express and admirable, in action how like an angel, in apprehension how like a god ; the beauty of the world, the paragon of animals."

Aphorism No. 1 is much more like Bunsby than like Shakespeare.

In his Short Notes he misuses words and uses repetition inexcusably. They are ungrammatical and discordantly awkward in construction. (The Rev. Mr. Abbot, in his introduction to Mrs. Pott's work on Bacon's Promus, says, " The errors in the Latin and Greek are Bacon's, and are of a nature to make Latin and Greek scholars uneasy.") It does not seem likely that errors of this kind, which are so noticeable, arise from carelessness, for he was a laborious and painstaking writer, nor is it supposable that he would have issued a paper of which he entertained doubts regarding its value and finish. My purpose is simply to suggest that the faults are in the nature of the man, and that in all his productions there is lacking the nice perception and rhythm of the poet.

In all probability Queen Elizabeth must have read his essay upon Masques and Triumphs. It was a critique upon an entertainment purely of the court, and therefore would only interest the court. As she was quite vain of her literary acquirements, and works on social accomplishments were the chief favourites in court society, his Short Notes would also naturally come under her attention. These two compositions would be alone sufficient ground for the Queen's disbelief in his ability. She judged him by evidence of such gifts as concern this inquiry ; naturally, a woman of her temperament, decision, and energy would not be favourably impressed with the powers of a man who condescended to write such oracular nonsense about the court festivities and who cultivated a habit of speaking "drawingly" on all occasions. His "Novum Organum" was published after her death and was dedicated to King James, who admitted that it was beyond his comprehension. He said of it, "It is like the peace of God that passeth understanding." In proof that the King's inability to understand this scientific work does not convict him of very dense stupidity, read the heading of one of the chapters of "Advancement of Learning."

"The art of judgment divided into induction and the syllogism—Induction developed in the Novum Organum—The syllogism divided into direct and inverse reduction—Inverse reduction divided into the doctrine of analytics and confutations—The division of the latter into confutations of sophisms, the unmasking of vulgarisms (equivocal terms), and the destruction of delusive images or idols—Delusive appearances divided into idola tribus, idola specus and idola fori—Appendix to the art of judgment—The adapting the demonstration to the nature of the subject." This was all in Latin, and it is doubtful if a trio of men in the kingdom knew what it meant.

In the "Novum Organum" Bacon invented a nomenclature suited to his fancy of the subject, but so rude and inappropriate as never to have been accepted by any others, such as "Idols of the Tribe," "Idols of the Den," "Idols of the Market," and "Idols of the Theatre," to describe races, individuals, commerce and false theories. Under the latter head he included everything not his own—in his own words, "All the systems of philosophy hitherto received or imagined." He also originated such terms as "twitching instances" and "lancing instances," because the former "twitched the understanding" and the latter "pierced nature." King James' frank avowal apparently cost him no blushes. To have affected an understanding of the work or an interest in it, would only have made him singular, perhaps ridiculous. Macaulay says, "The faults of James, both as a man and a prince, were numerous, but insensibility to the claims of genius and learning was not among them."

Ben Jonson in his "Discoveries," after stating that few could get beyond the introduction to this work, says, "It is a book." It was called the "Novum Organum" because it was intended to supplant Aristotle's "Organon," and was first published in 1620, during a period when, by the assertions of his friends, he was too busy with political affairs to spare time to write plays. As a further rebuttal of that assumption it may be stated that he held no office under the government for the last six years of his life, but spent all his time in literary pursuits. The "Novum Organum" was issued just prior to this period of retirement.

The tone of his speculative works drew forth the criticism that he "wrote philosophy like a Lord Chancellor," and Coke said of his "Novum Organum"

"It deserves not to be read in schools,
But to be freighted in the ship of fools."

which simile was suggested by a device on the title-page, of a ship passing the Pillars of Hercules. The legal bent of his mind was so strong that he could not, or would not, drop its idiom even in his philosophic and scientific works, and when he attempted narrative—as in the "New Atlantis"—he adopted a scriptural phraseology as suited to the gravity of his mind and fancy.

In book VI., Devey Edition, "Advancement of Learning," Bacon treats of method of speech, wisdom of delivery, etc. Rhetoric he calls "traditive prudence," and says of it, "A third collection wanting to the apparatus of rhetoric is what we call lesser forms, and these are a kind of portals, postern doors, outer rooms, back rooms, and passages of speech, which may serve indifferently for all subjects, such as prefaces, conclusions, digressions, transitions, etc. For, as in a building, a good distribution of the frontispiece, staircases, doors, windows, entries, passages and the like is not only agreeable but useful, so in speeches, if the accessories or underparts be decently and skilfully contrived and placed, they are of great ornament and service to the whole structure of the discourse."

This is certainly the "apparatus" of rhetoric and is mechanical to the plainest degree. It is a most ordinary conception of the subject of elegant literature. It would, in these times, excite the ridicule of a boy's schoolmates. It is too dull for Shakespeare's fools. If Shakespeare had written about the doors, windows, back rooms, and staircases of speech, he would have put it in the mouth of a Dogberry and would have mingled some drollery with it, to make its absurdity amusing.

Bacon's historians say he considered even the versification of the psalms a "culpable waste of time;" yet one "great student" (at least) is not influenced by such testimony, and he is said to have accumulated tons of evidence to prove not only that he wrote plays greater in volume than his scientific works, but that he had the time, patience and ingenuity to insert an arithmetical device in them to attest his authorship.

It would not be more incongruous to suppose Beethoven running a drum movement, containing some occult alphabetical symbol, through his symphonies, than to imagine that such compositions as Shakespeare's could be accompanied by anything so cheap and mechanical. Some even go to Shakespeare's grave to find evidence of Bacon's work. If such testimony were to be found in an epitaph, how much more reasonable it would be to look for it at Bacon's tomb. An inscription containing a cipher that would reveal a secret, might have been placed there without attracting any attention, which could not have been done at Stratford; but, instead of such a scheme, this is what Devey says of his grave : "He was buried in St. Michael's Church, St. Albans, by the side of his mother. A monument was soon after erected to his memory by his secretary, Sir Thomas Meantys, which represents him in a sitting posture, with an inscription which strangely parodies the sublime opening of the instauration, 'Franciscus Bacon,

Baro de Verulam, St. Albani Viccomes . . . sic sedebat'" (sat thus).

"A stranger standing over the grave of the great regenerator of physical science might fairly expect to be entertained with something better than a pun upon one of the most striking passages in his writings."

The cipher theory is too absurd for serious thought, but there are people—including its inventor—who evidently do not appreciate its mechanical difficulties. It would be impossible for anyone but a printer to arrange a cipher upon a printed sheet. The printed page and the manuscript vary greatly from each other; but for the purpose of such a device all inaccuracy would have to be absolutely avoided. If such a thing were *possible*, it could not be done without the full aid and co-operation of the printer. It would require an immense amount of revision, alteration, time, labour and conference with the author, and no one could carry through such a scheme and conceal it from the compositor. We know absolutely that there was nothing of this in 1623. It is singular that anyone should find it easier to accept such a flimsy and impracticable theory than to recognize the simple fact of Shakespeare's genius.

The history of the plays heightens its impracticability. Appleton's Encyclopædia says, "Of Shakespeare's thirty-seven plays, seventeen were printed separately in quartos, in almost every instance without his co-operation and in many instances from copies surreptitiously obtained. The text of most of these quarto copies is very corrupt and imperfect. In 1623 two of his fellow actors, John Heminge and Henry Condell, superintended the publication of the first collected edition of his Comedies, Histories and Tragedies, from which, however, Pericles was omitted. This volume, known as the first folio, contains the only authentic text of Shakespeare's plays. But its authority is grievously impaired by the careless manner in which it was printed, and by the fact that in some cases it was put in type from the surreptitious and imperfect quartos which it was intended to supersede, and the errors which it not infrequently perpetuates ; but it corrects vastly more errors than it repeats and it supplies many deficiencies, although it leaves many to be supplied. Plainly, too, most of the quarto copies from which it was printed had been used as stage copies by Shakespeare's company, and thus received many corrections which were at least quasi authoritative. Of the text of twenty of the plays it is the only source. The text of Shakespeare's works, excepting his poems, was left in so corrupt a state by the early printers, that, the author's manuscript having perished, it needed much editorial care to bring it even into a tolerably sound condition."

It must be borne in mind that when this folio edition was printed Shakespeare had been dead seven years. It was at least twelve years since the last play was written, and some of these plays were thirty years old. Bacon was at his house at Gorhambury, in disgrace, forbidden the precincts of the court. His sentence was proclaimed in 1621, and not till 1624 was it entirely remitted. It cannot then, by any possibility, be supposed that he had the most remote agency in the printing of the folio edition which it is claimed contains a device of such exactness as to the paging and the number of words contained on the pages, that by some manner of use, a story is disclosed which proves that this man, forbidden to come within the verge of the court, wrote Shakespeare's plays, and superintended their publication, without any one disclosing, or even knowing the secret, this too, in collusion with the devoted friends of Shakespeare, who had such difficulty in gathering and collating his works, that it required years to complete the task. It is proper here to direct attention to the fact that it is this folio edition of the plays that the inventor of the cipher depends upon for the kernel of his story, and to draw attention to the absurdity and weakness of the assumption, that Heminge and Condell, the loving friends of Shakespeare, joined a ruined man, then under the deepest public disgrace, in the knavery of imbedding with their work, a wicked defamation of their friend, and inserting with it a key to its future revelation. A quotation from the preface to their publication reveals the entire absence of any connection between them and Bacon, or of any suspicion on their part that the author of the plays might be then living. "It had bene a thing, we confesse, worthy to have bene wished, that the author himselfe had liv'd to set forth, and overseen his owne writings, but since it hath been ordain'd otherwise, **and he by death departed from that right,** we pray you not to envie his friends the office of their care, and paine." It would be a heavy bribe that could seduce the reverential love of these men to betray its object. Bacon was then in deep penury, as well as disgrace.

It is a satisfaction that history fixes the whereabouts of Bacon just at this time. Probably there was then no man more notorious than he. He was scheming to get back into office, misrepresenting instances of celebrated men in history in order to make his offence less culpable, utterly without shame, and his successor trying his utmost to defeat him. The plays were collected and published during that time. Twenty of them had never been published, some had been in print as much as thirty years, and for many years were used upon the stage. The printers cut them, and Shakespeare's two friends did their utmost to put them in print as nearly perfect as possible. It is common to hear regrets that Shakespeare did not publish his plays, so, that we might have them in perfect form : now, we have a theory, that even the careless usage that they received, the years of knocking about the theatre, the uncertainty as to the genuine and the spurious, and the cutting and slashing by the printers, have not even altered or changed the text enough to dislocate a cipher that existed in the manuscript. Many of the plays, and notably too, those which it is claimed furnish this arithmetical device, had not been in manuscript for twenty years, but had passed through an intermediate publication. When it is considered that the disarrangement of a single word would destroy the whole fabric, and that all tnese requirements must be accurately observed by people who did not even suspect that such a weighty secret existed, it must be considered the most extraordinary mechanical coincidence that ever happened. There is but one way of explaining it, and that is, that its ingenuity was so miraculous that no accident or design could destroy it.

While Bacon's authentic writings exist, no cipher or arithmetical device can show him capable of producing the plays. If in some musty archives his sworn affidavit should be found asserting his authorship of the plays, still would be heard his limping, shackled verse of the 104th Psalm. It is not a cipher that is needed to make a Shakespeare of Bacon. It is some evidence, primarily, that he possessed to any degree the incomparable poetic fancy and dramatic genius of Shakespeare. If he had desired to lay claim to the plays, he was too shrewd a lawyer to have chosen a means so uncertain and difficult as that. He was not wanting in cunning and strategy, and could have easily contrived a plan to explode the mystery of his dramatic gifts, when the gifts from princes could be no longer enjoyed. To his champions, however, inconsistency, improbability, or stupidity, have no weight.

"The cipher" undertakes the task of adding even more than Shakespeare to Bacon, for this theory ascribes to Bacon also the divination to foresee that a man would appear who could and would work out the puzzle. The enigma, of course, would be of no use unless some one could solve it, and thus might easily defeat its own object. Considering how many easier and common-sense ways might be devised to disclose a posthumous secret, the choice of such an uncertain and extraordinary one needs explanation. This perhaps, is furnished by the assumption of Bacon's faith in the zeal and cleverness of one for centuries yet unborn.

The first impression created by this vagary might easily be, that it was a piece of pastime, and that its author looked more for profit and notoriety from the novelty of his proposition, than for reputation through its success, but when accompanied by the invention of a loathsome story having no foundation in fact, or historical support, the mind marvels for a key to the motive that could suggest such a malicious prank, or impel such wanton and reckless trifling with the reputation of any man, living or dead. To the lovers of poetic imagery, who read the plays with inexpressible delight, and wonder at their continuously new discovered beauty and truth, it seems shocking that such effort should be devoted to proving them merely the vehicle for conveying to posterity, the hidden record of an obscene scandal. What a reflection upon Bacon such a monstrous assumption is, can only be conceived when the exalted position he occupied is compared with that of the humble poet, and the paltry purpose of handing down to future ages such a tale of disgrace to a poor actor, is compared with the laborious and artful means employed by a great man to transmit it. The cipher indicates in its author, a nature, to Bacon's "A little more than kin and less than kind."

If the story said to be told by the cipher were true, and contained in the plays, it would be the only reason why Bacon should have been ashamed of them, but then it would be the most powerful argument against "the cipher." If he was sincere in his dying wish, that he might be thought well of by posterity —and no one will doubt it—he would have been careful to leave no clue to connect him with the discovery of such childish and disgraceful employment of his powers. Much as has been said to the detriment of Bacon, by critics, no one has yet imputed to him anything so vulgar, wicked and senseless as this story of his latest champion. It is a shameless defamation of Bacon as well as of Shakespeare.

If this author's book would be generally read there would be no need of other refutation, but its ponderosity and the noise that has accompanied it, may, like those attributes of Bacon's works, impress public belief with an erroneous estimate of its force. A slight sketch of its character as deciphered by the writer, is therefore not out of place here. The author begins with an invented story, then roams through the plays to find words to represent it, he then, by the use of movable factors that have no coherence with any system, or any fundamental basis for existence, proceeds to force the result already determined upon. That he fixes the conclusion before finding evidence to support it, is so apparent, that no one would expect him to find anything not in accord with his scheme, or to disclose it if he did. If in his endless combinations of "roots and modifiers" and the ever convenient representative "x," he should stumble upon something that controverted the theory he is seeking to build up, there is no compulsion upon him to pursue that trail further, or to announce his failure. How many sturdy barriers of this kind confronted him in his struggle to distort the plays into a mask for scurrility, the public will never learn. A new root for a starting point, a different treatment of the hyphens and compounds, with moderate complaisance upon the part of "x," would circumvent all such obstacles, and open a new road to the object. It must be evident to anyone, and doubtless is well known to its inventor, that the same process applied to Bacon's works would produce like results; their imperfect Latin would offer the most serious difficulty. It would have been fatal to "the cipher" to have announced the factors upon which it is based, before the completion of the work of elaborating it.

It has been the almost invariable rule of the Baconites to smutch the plays as well as Shakespeare. The stress laid upon the lack of high education, and upon the youthful peccadilloes of the great bard, has been frequently supplemented by disparagement of the morality and worth of the poems, as well as of their originality. These need no defence here, they have a voice potent in itself. The flimsy argument that a boyish misdemeanour evidences a lack of the soul and spirit that inspired the muse, is refuted by the very relation of the means Shakespeare adopted in retaliation for the penalty imposed upon him. No stronger indication of his natural bent, and the direction his genius imparted to his acts, could be given, than the fact that he sweetened his revenge by posting verses upon his enemy. The records of some of the most illustrious writers of poety witness, that genius of that order does not dwell only with the highest morality or chastity; but, if the counter proposition were true, and thus the shortcomings of Shakespeare were an insuperable bar to his title to the authorship of the plays, with what redoubled weight must this argument apply to Bacon. Shakespeare may have been indifferent to portions of the moral code that do not imply a heart untouched by sympathy, or a soul dead to sentiment and to truth, but he was never venal, or mendacious; qualities that could not harbour in a soul inspired by the living truth and its beauteous images, everywhere depicted by his facile pen. There is no need of an artfully concealed and miraculously discovered cipher, to disclose the flagitious nature that distinguishes the man to whom the author of the mystic key to Shakespeare, would transfer the laurels of the traduced bard. It is surprising that anyone should desire to attribute the sublimest creation in literature to one whom Pope styles the "meanest of mankind." If indications and proofs of the genius and poetic power of Bacon were abundant and irrefutable, rational judgment would not concede that a man of his nature and propensities could create the characters of Shakespeare, and put into their utterances, a philosophy and sentiment so utterly unlike anything in Bacon's life, or in his published works. A man who is supposed by Macaulay, to have carried his venality so far, as to accept bribes from both sides of a litigation, and who in some cases had not the honour to perform the service to which he sold himself. It would be impossible to reason, and to natural laws, that such a being could have had the most remote connection with the plays, and equally impossible to retain an undiminished pleasure in them, if such a fallacy received the seal of truth.

Macaulay, in his essay on Bacon, endeavoured to be just to him, but it is a terrible arraignment of his character. He says, "When accused of accepting bribes, he assured his friends in the strongest terms of his innocence. He afterwards confessed his guilt, and begged the lords to be merciful to a broken reed. He admitted that he had no defence, and submitted his confession, and said, 'It is my act, my hand, my heart.' Mr. Montague has laboured hard to prove his confession to have been a falsehood on his part, made at the request of the king. He assures us that Bacon was innocent, and that he had the means of making a perfectly satisfactory defence, and that when he plainly and ingenuously confessed that he was guilty of corruption, and when he afterwards solemnly affirmed that his confession was his act, his hand, his heart, he was telling a great lie, and that he refrained from bringing forth proofs of his innocence because he durst not disobey the king and the favourite who for selfish objects pressed him to plead guilty. It seems strange that Mr. Montague should not perceive that, while attempting to vindicate Bacon's reputation, he is really casting on it the foulest of all aspersions. He imputes to his idol a degree of meanness and depravity more loathsome than judicial corruption. A corrupt judge may have many good qualities; but a man who, to please a powerful patron, solemnly declares himself guilty of corruption, when he knows himself to be innocent, must be a monster of servility and impudence."

Bacon presided at the torture of the poor

old clergyman, Peacham, whom he was prosecuting for treason, and against whom no evidence existed except a few sheets of loose manuscript, which were accidentally found in his home when the constables broke in to search for proof of libel upon his bishop. They were not even intended for publication, and had never been preached, but were simply the poor man's private thoughts in justification of his resistance to tyranny. Bacon fell upon him, and pursued him to his death. He used all his ingenuity, even to tampering with the judges, to secure the conviction of the old man, and he succeeded. The government, however, from "very shame at the futility of the charges," did not carry out the sentence, but the man languished and died in prison. His record in this persecution is simply atrocious. Macaulay says, "In order to convict Peacham, it was necessary to find facts as well as law. Accordingly this wretched old man was put to the rack, and while undergoing the horrible infliction, was examined by Bacon, but in vain. No confession could be wrung out of him, and Bacon wrote to the king, complaining that Peacham had a dumb devil." One of the sentences in

Bacon's collection of Ornamenta Rationalia reads "Pain makes even the innocent man a liar," but Peacham proved an exception. If the old man had been a dangerous character, and Bacon had been actuated by an honest desire to serve the state, it would even then have been revolting for one in his position to go to the Tower to practice such sickening cruelty upon a suspected old man ; but when we know that Bacon laboured to influence the judges to assist him in the prosecution, and that among his printed papers there is an admission that pain extorts lies, and not the truth, from the innocent, and when the fact is considered that the government sympathized so little with his servile zeal as to refuse to carry out its own sentence, his mercenary and heartless character in the pursuit of court favour is exposed. Yet this merciless inquisitor has a following who seem to believe, and wish to lead others into the belief, that he wrote

> "The quality of mercy is not strained.
> It droppeth as the gentle rain from heaven
> Upon the place beneath. It is twice blest.
> It blesseth him that gives and him that takes.
> It is mightiest in the mightiest. It becomes
> The throned monarch better than his crown.

> His sceptre shows the force of temporal power,
> The attribute to awe and majesty
> Wherein doth sit the dread and fear of kings ;
> But mercy is above this sceptred sway.
> 'Tis enthroned in the hearts of kings.
> It is an attribute of God himself,
> And earthly power doth then show likest God's
> When mercy seasons justice."

Never has there been a scrap of evidence to show that the poet who wrote those lines had any fellowship or personal acquaintance with Bacon : nothing so discreditable has ever been shown of him. If theories that have only supposable probability for a foundation were admissible, I might suggest the influence of Bacon about the court as one of the causes that shortened Shakespeare's career on the stage, and decided his return to Stratford, or that out of Bacon's inability to compose such dramatic plays as were then popular at court, arose the provocation for his disparaging and contemptuous allusions to them.

Macaulay's well-known depth of research, comprehensive grasp of facts and details, and his calm method of presenting honest conclusions, renders him preëminent as a safe authority. It is for this reason that his testimony is here cited at some length. He says of

Bacon: "His faults were—we write it with pain —coldness of heart and meanness of spirit. He seems to have been incapable of feeling strong affection, of facing great dangers, of making great sacrifices. His desires were set on things below. Wealth, precedence, titles, patronage, the mace, the seals, the coronet, large houses, fair gardens, rich manors, massive service of plate, gay hangings, curious cabinets had as great attractions for him as for any of the courtiers who dropped on their knees in the dirt when Elizabeth passed by, and then hastened home to write to the king of Scots that her grace seemed to be breaking fast. For these objects he stooped to everything and endured everything. For these he had sued in the humblest manner; and, when unjustly and ungraciously repulsed, had thanked those who had repulsed him, and had begun to sue again. For these objects as soon as he found that the smallest show of independence in Parliament was offensive to the queen, he had abased himself in the dust before her, and implored forgiveness in terms better suited to a convicted thief than a knight of the shire. For these he joined and for these he forsook

Lord Essex. He continued to plead his patron's cause with the queen as long as he thought that by pleading that cause he might serve himself. Nay, he went further; for his feelings, though not warm, were kind; he pleaded that cause as long as he thought he could plead it without injury to himself. But when it became evident that Essex was going headlong to his ruin, Bacon began to tremble for his own fortunes. What he had to fear would not have been very alarming to a man of lofty character. It was not death. It was not imprisonment. It was the loss of court favour. It was the being left behind by others in the career of ambition. When once he had determined to act against his friend, knowing himself to be suspected, he acted with more zeal than would have been necessary or justifiable if he had been employed by a stranger. He exerted his professional talents to shed the earl's blood, and his literary talents to blacken the earl's memory."

Notwithstanding the powerful influence of Essex with the Queen, years of persistent importunity in Bacon's behalf was entirely fruitless, and he gave Bacon Twickenham

Court (a place so beautiful that Bacon called it Garden of Paradise) simply in compensation for his disappointment at not being able to procure him some government post that had been vacant. He was under no obligation to him whatever, but Essex seems to have been the one man who for a long time had a sincere friendship for Bacon. This was purely the gift of a man of generous nature to another whose real character he did not suspect. When Bacon thought of making his fortune by marriage with a rich widow, Essex urged his suit; after that, in the trials, he attacked Essex—who was not allowed counsel—with such venom that he interrupted Bacon and called upon him to quit the part of an advocate and come forward as a witness.

It is worthy of mention that Shakespeare's friend—the Earl of Southampton—to whom he dedicated his Venus and Adonis and Lucrece—was arraigned, convicted and sentenced with the Earl of Essex. The queen spared Southampton's life, and he was a prisoner in the Tower at the time of her death. He was liberated upon the accession of James to the English throne. It does not add anything to the probability of mercantile transactions or secret understandings, between Shakespeare and Bacon, that Bacon should have been in this political episode, such an active and mortal enemy of Shakespeare's friend and patron, the man to whom it is evident he was more attached and desirous of expressing devotion, than to any other.

Macaulay says further: " He was one of the last of the tools of power who persisted in a practice the most barbarous and the most absurd that has ever disgraced jurisprudence, of a practice of which, in the preceding generation, Elizabeth and her ministers had been ashamed. The practice of torturing prisoners was then generally acknowledged to be illegal, and was execrated by the public as barbarous. Queen Elizabeth in her reign had issued an order positively forbidding the torturing of prisoners under any pretence whatever. Bacon far behind his age! Bacon clinging to exploded abuses! Bacon withstanding the progress of improvement! Bacon struggling to push back the human mind."

During the time he held the great seal he was the willing instrument of a ring of public plunderers, and granted infamous monopolies to the court favourites, equal to any of the like modern conspiracies that have become notorious. Macaulay thus refers to the fact, "Having assisted the patentees to obtain this monopoly Bacon assisted them also in the steps which they took to guard it. He committed several people to close confinement for disobeying his tyrannical edicts. The patentees were armed with powers as great as have ever been given to farmers of the revenue in the worst governed countries. They were authorized to search houses and arrest interlopers, and these formidable powers were used for purposes viler than even those for which they were given—for the wreaking of old grudges and for the corrupting of female chastity. The man who stooped to render such services to others was not likely to be scrupulous as to the means by which he enriched himself. He and his dependents accepted large presents from persons who were engaged in chancery suits. The amount of plunder which he collected in this way it is impossible to estimate. There can be no doubt that he received much more than was proved on the trial, though it may be less than was suspected by the public. His enemies stated his gains at a hundred thousand pounds, but this was probably an exaggeration."

On one occasion, when Bacon felt well assured of his place, he ventured to meddle in some private matter of Buckingham's. He immediately discovered his mistake, and sought with the most sickening servility to regain Buckingham's favour.

Macaulay says of this, "It is said that on two successive days Bacon repaired to Buckingham's house, that on two successive days he was suffered to remain in an ante-chamber among foot boys, seated on a wooden box, with the great seal of England at his side, and that at length, when he was admitted, he flung himself on the floor, kissed the favourite's feet, and vowed never to rise until he was forgiven."

His own historian says in the introduction to his works, "**He could see nothing except through the senses, and was disposed to undervalue everything that did not contribute to physical enjoyment or tangible glory.**"

The introduction alluded to says elsewhere, " Bacon even entertained hopes of resuming his seat in the Lords, if not on the Woolsack, and did not scruple in his letters to James to pervert history, with a view to establish similar cases of disintegration. 'Demosthenes,' says Bacon in one of these communications, 'was banished for bribery of the highest nature, yet was recalled with honour. Marcus Lucius was condemned for exactions, yet afterwards made consul and censor. Seneca was banished for divers corruptions, yet was afterwards restored, and an instrument in the memorable Quinquenium Neronis.'"

It is not a pleasing task to copy a mass of detail of such discreditable nature, and to show the weak and unworthy side of a man's character, particularly of a man who was so anxious that in future, at least, his name should be honoured, and who in his will appealed to the kind judgment of mankind, "For my name and memory, I leave it to men's charitable speeches, to foreign nations and to the next generation." In one sense especially it is not agreeable; that is, that it is done in refutation of a claim that, personally, he never made. The authorities quoted are, however, well known to every one interested in Bacon, for they are those who have written his life and arranged and edited his works. They are all in some respects his admirers, and none deny his learning or mental capacity. Spedding's much qualified praise of his undeveloped "poetic passion" is not intended as any disparagement of his real gifts, for Spedding knew that Bacon made no claim to dramatic talent, but that he considered it (in his own language) "a culpable waste of time" in a man of such scientific attainments, and Spedding apparently approved.

Bacon's political career is a matter of history and is easily found. It, and the philosophy of his essays and speculative works, with all the facts and information that can be obtained as to the character, habits, interests, associations and employments of the two men, have a material and indissoluble connection with the subject, if in determining the authorship we are to ignore the fact of Shakespeare's admitted and undisputed title to it during his own and Bacon's life, and are to resolve the question merely upon the possible workings and capabilities of two human minds ; if we are to cast out concurrent facts and substitute conjecture, if we are to discard the real and adopt the visionary, if instead of a rational belief in the testimony of Shakespeare's co-labourers, we are to assume the mythical and miraculous theory of the Baconians.

My object is to present Bacon by his own writings, by his biographers, his acts and his critics; to suggest the conclusions and impressions that these authorities and evidences convey to the mind, and to invite those interested, to an examination of the same data.

The extracts which I have made, and the facts which I have exposed, represent him fairly. He was a man of limited fancy, earthly taste, mechanical imagination, material sense and selfish purpose.

These are not the qualities that anyone attributes to Shakespeare, or that are betrayed in any of his works.

CHAPTER IV.

Bacon as a "soaring angel"—Advice to the person who has incurred the displeasure of his prince—Thrift that follows fawning—Extracts from various essays—Essay on the True Greatness of Kingdoms—His attitude toward the civilization of his time.

WHILE Macaulay heaps every reproach that language permits upon Bacon's character and conduct, he credits him with very different qualities as a student. He says, "The difference between the soaring angel and the creeping snake was but a type of the difference between Bacon the philosopher and Bacon the attorney-general,—Bacon seeking truth and Bacon seeking the seals. Those who survey only one half of his character may speak of him with unmixed admiration or unmixed contempt. In his library all his rare powers were under the guidance of an honest ambition, of an enlarged philanthropy, of a sincere love of truth." I have copied this because I think it unjust to cite that which is so scathing and to omit what qualifies it on the other side.

If it is true that Bacon's writings were so pure, while his acts were deserving of "unmixed contempt," then some of the assertions here made may do him injustice. I would not presume to dispute the judgment of the great essayist, but I may produce some of these writings in evidence of conclusions not at all in agreement with this idea. One cannot believe in such a dual nature, and cannot understand how a man's out-of-door exploits can be so vile while his studies are so angelic, as naturally the latter is the preparation for the former.

In Bacon's Advancement of Learning there is an article upon the way in which a man should act who wishes to regain the favour of his superior, which follows so closely some of Macaulay's descriptions of his servility as to furnish an instance of what is here meant.

"'If the displeasure of great men rise up against thee, forsake not thy place; for pliant behaviour extenuates great offences' (Prov. 29 : 11).

"This aphorism shows how a person ought to behave when he has incurred the displeasure of his prince. The precept hath two parts—

(1) that the person quit not his post, and (2) that he with diligence and caution apply to the cure as of a dangerous disease. For when men see their prince incensed against them, what through impatience of disgrace, fear of renewing the wound by sight, and partly to let their prince behold their contrition and humiliation, it is usual for them to retire from their office or employ, and sometimes to resign their places and dignities into their prince's hands. But Solomon disparages this method as pernicious. For (1) it publisheth the disgrace too much; whence both our enemies and enviers are more emboldened to hurt us, and our friends the more intimidated from lending us their assistance. (2) By this means the anger of the prince, which perhaps would have blown over of itself had it not been made public, becomes more fixed; and having now begun to displease the person, ends not but in his downfall. (3) The resigning carries something of ill will with it, and shows a dislike of the times, which adds the evil of indignation to that of suspicion. The following remedies regard the cure: (1) Let him above all things beware how by any insensibility or elation of mind he seems re-

gardless of his prince's displeasure or not affected as he ought. He should not compose his countenance to a stubborn melancholy, but to a grave and decent dejection; and show himself in all actions less brisk and cheerful than usual. It may also be for his advantage to use the assistance and mediation of a friend with the prince, seasonably to insinuate with how great a sense of grief the person in disgrace is inwardly affected. (2) Let him carefully avoid even the least occasions of reviving the thing which caused the displeasure, or of giving any handle to fresh distaste and open rebuke. (3) Let him diligently seek all occasions wherein his service may be acceptable to his prince, that he may both show a ready desire of retrieving his past offence, and his prince perceive what a servant he must lose if he quit him. (4) Either let him prudently transfer the blame upon others, or insinuate that the offence was committed with no evil desire, or show that their malice who accused him to the prince aggravated the thing above measure. (5) Lastly, let him in every respect be watchful and intent upon the cure."

It is impossible to read this article and make

it mean anything else than moral obliquity. It does not come under the head of either of the qualities ascribed by Macaulay to Bacon "in his library," and least of all is it a sincere "love of truth." On the contrary, without the slightest compunction, with no attempted casuistry, and apparently with no consciousness of the evil of the teaching, he advises the man who has incurred the "displeasure of his prince" to tell the meanest kind of a falsehood and put the blame on another. If there is any other way of reading such passages—and it would seem as though Bacon's admirers and some of his biographers possessed such a faculty—then it may be capable of a different construction, but as it is in such perfect accord with his life-long attitude toward his superiors, it seems reasonable that he meant it and believed it.

One can easily imagine him to have written it before starting out to wait upon Buckingham, and that he studied it again before going the second day to sit in the ante-room among the foot-boys.

It is questionable if any writer but Bacon ever descended to a study of the look a man should assume and the gait he should adopt in order to propitiate the displeasure of his prince. It was the lack of manliness, exposed here, which made it possible for him to thank those who "repulsed him and sue again," and the same absence of shame and truthfulness that permitted him to misrepresent historical characters, in order to invent precedents by which he hoped to brave out his disgrace and return to power and position. I may be allowed to suppose that Shakespeare, who probably knew Bacon's character thoroughly, had him in his thought when he wrote,

> "Let the candied tongue lick absurd pomp,
> And crook the pregnant hinges of the knee,
> Where thrift may follow fawning."

In nothing that he says is there a full reliance upon the sure return for a virtuous action or moral principle. He has no faith in character. The opening sentence in his Short Notes is a fair example of his foxy philosophy: "to deceive men's expectations generally (with cautel) argueth a staid mind and unexpected constancy." In plain meaning: Be on your guard. Conceal your real intentions. Never be frank, open, natural or straightforward. His philosophy is the science of outwitting others; and much of his essays is simply lessons in craft, artifice and finesse.

In his Essay on Discourse he say, "If you dissemble sometimes your knowledge of that you are thought to know, you shall be thought, another time, to know that you know not."

Essay on Fortune: "Certainly, there be not two more fortunate properties than to have a little of the fool and not too much of the honest."

On Negotiation: "If you would work any man, you must either know his nature and fashions, and so lead him; or his ends, and so persuade him; or his weaknesses and disadvantages, and so awe him; or those that have an interest in him, and so govern him."

Essay on Ceremonies and Respects: "It is a good precept, generally, in seconding another, yet to add somewhat of one's own, as: if you will grant his opinion, let it be with some distinction; if you will follow his motion, let it be with condition; if you will allow his counsel, let it be with alleging further reason."

Every one who has had any experience in committees; in public bodies; will recognize this picture of the man who always wants to "add something of his own." He is the marplot of every body of men who try to accomplish any work, and the Baconian idea seems to be his way of making his influence felt.

I do not mean to say that Bacon does not dislike falsehood and admire truth, or that he does not commend virtue, but when he does so, it is not positively and without conditions, but with qualification and reservation. In his Essay on Truth he says, "Mixture of falsehood is like alloy in coin of gold and silver, which may make the metal work the better, but it embaseth it." In another passage, "Truth may perhaps come to the price of a pearl, that showeth best by day, but it will not rise to the price of a diamond or carbuncle, that showeth best in varied lights. A mixture of a lie doth ever add pleasure. Doth any man doubt, that if there were taken out of men's minds vain opinions, flattering hopes, false valuations, imaginations, as one would, and the like, but it would leave the minds of a number of men poor shrunken things, full of melancholy and indisposition, and unpleasing to themselves?" In another essay, "The best composition and temperament is to have an openness in fame and opinions, secrecy in habit, dissimulation in seasonable use, and a power to feign if there be no remedy."

The essays abound in these half-beliefs. That which is false may not be a creditable member of his moral family, but it is a useful one, and one that, in his opinion, he cannot afford to disown or turn out of doors; for in emergencies, such as that of the man who wants to "cure as of a dangerous disease" and does not want to lose his place, it may, in the end, be the only thing that will save him.

In his Essay on Cunning he is so much in sympathy with the subject that one is unable to determine how much of it is intended as commendation of the shifts, tricks and snares cited, and how much is simply descriptive of the quality. For instance, he says, "If a man would cross a business that he doubts some other would handsomely and effectually move, let him pretend to wish it well, and move it himself in such sort as may foil it." His letters to Essex contain advice of the same character; he writes, "*You may serve your turn by pretence of it, and stay it nevertheless.*"

Again, "*But I say keep it in substance, but abolish it in shows to the queen.*" Again, "Your lordship should never be without some particulars afoot, *which you should seem to pursue with earnestness and affection, and let them fall upon taking knowledge of her majesty's opposition and dislike.*"

Macaulay undoubtedly refers to the Novum Organum when he compares Bacon to the "soaring angel." It is a work of quite limited size, and treats of matters which cannot be compared with imaginative works. It is foreign also to any questions of political character, and in some places it contains the usual disparagement of works of fiction and the imagination. The evidence of Bacon's absorbing interest in it is everywhere evident, and there can be no doubt but that he supposed it would displace and supersede everything of the like character "hitherto received or imagined," which he described as "so many plays brought out and performed, creating fictitious and theatrical worlds." Yet his interest in peaceful arts and employments is qualified by such passages as the following, from his essays:

"It is certain that sedentary and within-door

arts, and delicate manufactures (that require rather the finger than the arm), have in their nature a contrariety to a military disposition ; and generally all warlike people are a little idle, and love danger better than travail, neither must they be too much broken of it if they shall be preserved in vigour : therefore it was great advantage in the ancient states of Sparta, Athens, Rome and others that they had the use of slaves, which commonly did rid those manufactures ; but that is abolished, in greatest part, by the Christian law. That which cometh nearest to it is to leave those arts chiefly to strangers (which, for that purpose, are to be more easily received), and to contain the principal bulk of the vulgar natives within those three kinds, tillers of the ground, free servants, and handicraftsmen of strong and manly arts ; as smiths, masons, carpenters, etc., not being professed soldiers."

Bacon's idea of the True Greatness of Kingdoms, which sets forth his principles on the subject of war and conquest, may not interest those who are simply looking for evidence of his relation to dramatic art, but this subject occupies a large place in Bacon's writings, it indicates his attitude toward the civilization of his time, and it properly belongs to a study of his character.

He wrote two papers for Buckingham in return for the remission of his sentence: one entitled Some Considerations touching a War with Spain, "in which he strives to excite the nation to make an unjustifiable attack upon an unoffending ally;" the other, An Advertisement touching an Holy War, "which was nothing more nor less than a dialogue upon the lawfulness of propagating religion by the sword." These were not in any sense angelic papers. The strongest argument put forth in them is the tempting treasures of gold and silver to be gained by such a conquest; and he cites the Castilian subjugation of Mexico, Peru, Chili, and parts of the West Indies, to make his motives clear. He was an advocate of war for itself, for conquest, for spoils, but condemned it for liberty. He says, "But above all for empires and greatness it importeth most that a nation do profess arms as their principal honour, study and occupation. No nation which doth not directly profess arms may look to have greatness fall into their mouths. Incident to this point is, for a state to have those laws or customs which may reach forth unto them just occasions (as may be pretended) of war, for there is that justice imprinted in the nature of man, that they enter not upon wars (whereof so many calamities do ensue) but upon some at least specious grounds and quarrels. The Turk hath at hand for cause of war the propagation of his law or sect, a quarrel that he may always command. The Romans, though they esteemed the extending the limits of their empire to be a great honour to their generals when it was done, yet they never rested upon that alone to begin a war. First, therefore, let nations that pretend to greatness have this, that they be sensible of wrongs, either upon borderers, merchants or politic ministers, and that they set not too long upon a provocation; secondly, let them be pressed and ready to give aid and succours to their confederates as it ever was with the Romans; insomuch, as if the confederate had leagues defensive with divers other states, and upon invasion offered did implore their aids severally, yet the Romans would ever be the foremost and leave it to none other to have the honour. As for wars which were anciently made on the behalf of a kind of party or tacit conformity of estate, I do not see how they can be well justified; as when the Romans made a war for the liberty of Græcia, or when the Lacedemonians and Athenians made wars to set up or pull down democracies or oligarchies, or when wars were made by foreigners under the pretence of justice, or protection to deliver the subjects of others from tyranny and oppression and the like. No body can be healthful without exercise, neither natural body nor politic, and certainly to a kingdom or estate a just and honourable war is the true exercise."

Of the spoils he says, "The triumphs of the generals upon their return, the great donatives and largesses upon the disbanding of the armies, were things able to inflame all men's courage, but above all, that of the triumph amongst the Romans was not pageants or gaudery, but one of the wisest and noblest institutions that ever was, for it contained three things: honour to the general, riches to the treasury out of the spoils, and donatives to the army; but that honour, perhaps, were not fit for monarchies, except it be in the person of the monarch himself, or his sons, as it came to pass in the times of the Roman emperors, who did impropriate the actual triumphs to themselves and their sons for such wars as they did achieve in person, and left only for wars achieved by subjects some triumphal garment and ensigns to the general."

The same idea even more grossly expressed will be found in the Advancement of Learning, under the title of "A Readiness for War Necessary." By many it is claimed for Bacon that he was a reformer and a philanthropist. No barbarian could have framed a policy better suited to satisfy the instincts of savages than this essay. It is not war for cause or for defence, or for justice. He says he cannot justify war for liberty or against oppression, or by foreigners under the pretence of justice, or to set up democracies. He advocates war as a profession, for military glory, for conquest and spoils, simply to destroy your neighbours and strengthen and enrich yourselves. He advises that there shall be at least a specious pretence of justification—not for the cause of justice, however, but to deceive those who fight better for a principle than without it. It is not a pretence of justice and liberty that he wants, but some imagined offence. He furnishes a list of pretexts for wars of such a nature, that no government seeking a quarrel need ever be without a provocation, *i.e.*, the propagation of sects, offences against politic ministers, against merchants, and the broils between the nation's allies and enemies. Bacon was an ideal politic minister for such a purpose, and the papers he wrote when his life was almost spent, show what causes for bloodshed he could have been depended upon to foment. His historians say of his effort to inaugurate a religious war, "The king certainly had his hands full in trying to extirpate heresies, reconcile schisms and reform manners; but our author was inclined to think a war might be undertaken at the same time." The ring of plunderers to whom he granted the patents, would at any time have discovered an offence and furnished "the specious ground and just occasions as might be pretended;" in fact it was for the chief of them that he made his argument.

The crowning figure of his harangue, however, which he calls "one of the noblest and wisest things that ever was," is the victorious army disbanding and dividing the plunder. He says, "These are such great and dazzling things in the eyes of mortals, as to be capable of firing the most frozen spirits and inflaming them for war." No doubt but that such a sight and such rewards would incite the worst passions of the lowest order of men, but what a heartless and infamous motive to be described as one of the "noblest and wisest things that ever was"! The wisdom and nobility of such a sight could only appear to a man of the same nature and instincts as the soldiers he describes.

Bacon's life was passed in a time of the most inhuman sectarian strife. He was twelve years old when the massacre of St. Bartholomew's day took place, and thirteen when the Duke of Alva returned from his frightful holy war in the Netherlands. The horrors of "an holy war" and its adjunct the Inquisition, were known to Bacon almost, if not actually, as an eye-witness, but instead of filling him with abhorrence, and ranging him on the side of humanity and progress, he regarded it as the true greatness of the kingdom.

Forbidden to come within the verge of the court, and an old man, he spent his time trying to tempt the greed of the nation, by the same arguments that are contained in his essays, to begin anew the bloody work. Even the mean old Roman emperor who with his sons "impropriated" the booty and gave the general nothing but some garments and ensigns is readily justified. He was in most willing accord with the worst spirits of his age, and wrote of Henry VIII. as "one of the goodliest persons of his time." He uttered no protest or even regret at the abuse of power, but led in the wicked race and set up the fiercest examples of barbarism as the true glory of the people. He was without the "dint of pity" or "touch of nature" that makes the "whole world kin."

If he had possessed any of the gentle nature that breathes in Shakespeare's poetry, instead of exulting over such a scene as the return of the red-handed soldiers loaded with their reeking plunder, he would, in imagination, have retraced the march of the marauders until he reached the ruined homes of the stricken enemy, and would have grieved at the degradation of human nature that could make such cruelty possible. If in these days it is thought that the benighted condition of the people in the fourteenth and fifteenth centuries was the cause of the savage dispositions of their rulers, Bacon knew better. He was familiar with noble examples in Greek and Roman history, and when he wanted an instance to compare with the queen's peaceful death, he could quickly recall Pius Antoninus, who lived and ruled fourteen hundred years before Bacon's time. It was because such examples of virtue, justice and wisdom did not move his admiration, and not from his ignorance of them, that he preferred the worst pagan examples to incite the Christians of his time to destroy each other.

CHAPTER V.

Bacon's interpretation of "A just man is merciful to his beast," etc.—His Essay on Deformity—His interpretation of another proverb—His habit of generalization—His Essay on Friendship—Mode of treatment for the human mind—His Essay on Love—His corpuscular study of Cupid.

IT was natural for Bacon to see everything in its bearing upon his political interests. He was continually an applicant for office and in nervous fear of incurring the displeasure of those in power above him. His personal interests were so urgent that they coloured everything he saw; consequently the subjects that he treats he brings down to the plane of his personal wants. They furnish the morals for his essays and interpret the lessons which the proverbs convey to him. That which he reads has very little signification to him independent of the service it may be forced to perform in support of his schemes. His general theme is the duty of subjects to their princes, and servants to their masters, and the rules that he proposes are the same as those which he followed in his attendance upon his superiors. As he never believed in resigning, he easily found a meaning in one of Solomon's proverbs that accorded with his view, and taught him the art of a "grave and decent dejection" and the "prudent" false accusation.

As he found Solomon so fully in accord with his own views, as to how a man should debase himself in order to "apply to the cure as of a dangerous disease," it is not singular that he should also press him into his service in support of his political designs. The proverb that he selects to this end is, "A just man is merciful to his beast, but the mercies of the wicked are cruel." He comments upon it in this manner: "This comparison has some resemblance to that of a prince and his subjects. A great soul, the noblest part of creation, is ever compassionate. Nay, the Turks, though a cruel and bloody nation, give alms to brutes and suffer them not to be tortured. But, lest this principle might seem to countenance all kinds of compassion, Solomon wholesomely subjoins: That the mercies of the wicked are cruel: that is, when such great offenders are spared as ought to be cut off with the sword of justice." Whatever the real meaning of this saying may have been when it was uttered, it certainly was not that which Bacon has tried to draw from it. I have heard it explained in a way that is instructive, that contains a truth and gives mercy no uncertain meaning, viz., that the "wicked" is meant to describe him who by abuse has maimed and crippled his beast beyond usefulness, and made its life a burden to it, but being touched with some degree of pity, mercifully puts it to death to end its sufferings ; in contrast with the man who ever treats his beast humanely, or the one who, having killed the mother bird, out of compassion for the helpless little ones in the nest, puts them to death to save them from hunger and starvation.

It is not singular that Bacon should entirely miss the sense of mercy in it ; for one who could examine an old man on the rack and feel nothing but exasperation, disappointment and chagrin at his victim's fortitude, courage and endurance, could have no knowledge of such a quality, and it is not probable that he believed his interpretation of it to be its true intent, but was simply using his own ingenuity in rendering it to suit his personal objects. It may have been written when he was trying to destroy Essex, Southampton and their fellows indicted for treason, or when he found that the queen would not put Peacham to death. He was constantly engaged in ferreting out treason, and he wanted no "impunity" for "great offenders." His interpretation of it was calculated to save the fruits of his zeal as a servile tool for the court favourites, and he wanted authority to sustain his edicts; it was entirely such necessities that suggested Solomon as having put forth a warning against mercy, because he feared that the tender care of dumb animals might unduly soften men's natures and lead them into an unwillingness to apprehend and punish criminals.

In view of the jealous and vindictive character of many of the rulers of Bacon's time, and for centuries previous, nothing can be imagined more needless than a fear of the exercise of mercy, or of unmerited compassion. In Henry VIII.'s reign there were 70,000 people executed for violations of law; in the reign of Elizabeth the average of executions was about

400 a year. James I. burned heretics; it was common to brand and torture those only suspected, and political prisoners were not allowed counsel. Appleton's Encyclopœdia says, "The common people had generally no knowledge of many of the laws and penalties, but their ignorance was no defence. Even at the beginning of this century there were 160 offences punishable by death in England; for instance, stealing above the value of twelvepence, or maliciously tearing or defacing of the garments of a person passing in the street."

In Bacon's preface to "A Preparation for the Union of Laws," he says, "I have read, and read with delight, the Scottish Statutes, and some other collection of their laws; with delight I say, partly to see their brevity and propriety of speech, and partly to see them come so near to our laws." He then gives a list of the various crimes and their penalties, the resemblance to which in the Scottish laws, affords him so much delight. The first paragraph of the punishment for treason reads, "In treason, the corporal punishment is by drawing on hurdle from the place of prison to the place of execution, and by hanging and being cut down alive, bowelling and quartering, and in women by burning." It was under such laws that Bacon sought to convert the humane teachings of this proverb into an admonition against a sovereign's clemency. It was the "great offenders" that were his political rivals, meet for the sword of justice. Whereas the proverb says mercy of the wicked, Bacon reads it as the mercy of a prince toward great offenders. One would not misconstrue a precept in that way except with design. Suppose he should have applied it to his own case, as might have been done at a later period of his life. Then it would have been wicked in James I. to release him from the Tower and remit his fine, after he had been convicted of great crimes. Still the parallel is incomplete, for princes in those times did not spare subjects out of mercy and compassion, but from policy and self-interest.

It is not the question of the original meaning of the proverb that I wish to emphasize, but the bias and temper in the nature of him who explains it.

People of gentle nature and fine sensibilities, often discover meanings in texts and precepts which give them greater beauty and power than the author's original conception, others miss the true import and intended application, and simply degrade them to the plane of their own restricted vision. In this case, Bacon seeks to set forth the meaning and intent of a precept that had survived for ages as a lesson of charity and tenderness. The wide divergence of his interpretation from the plain meaning of the language, and especially from the benevolent construction given to it by the other example quoted, is pointedly suggestive as being the reflex of instincts confined to selfish limits, a mind capable of only sordid deliberations, and a heart impervious to the gentle impulses that gave life to the touching pathos, everywhere displayed in the plays, when suffering and mercy are the incidents portrayed. There is no moral, or purpose, pointed by the plays, that indicates in their author, any such attributes as must have impelled so cruel and tortuous an application as Bacon has given to this precept against the brutal exercise of power over the helpless.

The quality of mind most distant from a genius for delineation of character, is that which cannot detect individual traits, personal peculiarities, and the shades of difference which distinguish the person from the class, or which cannot drop its own personality and enter into that of its imagination.

This is a feature of the question of the authorship of the plays, not second to any other. How far Bacon was able to read the human mind, beyond the needs of a detective, which a suspicion of courtiers' motives taught him, may be learned from some of his writings, in which he stamps people with mental and emotional qualities by the most thoughtless and arbitrary rules; for instance, in his Essay on Deformity he says, " Deformed persons are even with nature, for as nature hath done ill by them, so do they by nature; being for the most part (as the Scripture saith) void of natural affection, and so they have their revenge of nature. Whosoever hath anything fixed in his person that doth induce to contempt, hath also a personal spur in himself to rescue and deliver himself from scorn, therefore all deformed persons are extremely bold; first, as in their own defence, as being exposed to scorn, but in process of time by general habit. Also it stirreth in them industry, and especially of that kind to watch and observe the weakness of others that they may have something to repay." (Then follows the usual casting up of their chances of preferment by kings.) He speaks of them again in his Essay on Envy, "Deformed persons and old men and bastards are envious; for he that cannot possibly mend his own case will do what he possibly can to impair another's."

In the sense that I desire to notice this kind of writing, its worst fault is not its falsity, but that he should have had such a dull comprehension of his subject, as to suppose that the people whom he classes together were all of one pattern in such respects. The first thought suggested is that some aspirant at the court, of whom he was jealous, may have had personal defect. He was jealous of his cousin Robert Cecil; I have read that he was such a person. In all probability he knew the court jesters and their artificial life, and he carelessly imagined that all misshapen people were what they seemed to be. A small amount of observation would have taught him that physical deformity is no index to infirmity of character or disposition; that it is no more an indication of moral blemish than physical beauty is of the reverse. It is more fatal to his genius as an observer of human nature, to draw such a sweeping and erroneous picture of a numerous class of people from such a fault, than if he had been actuated by personal dislike.

The people who are so afflicted do not need champions now, and probably did not then. To say that they are all bold, revengeful, envious and "void of natural affection," everybody knows to be the flattest nonsense, and it is not at all improved by including all "old men" as "envious." There is nothing in his Essay on Deformity worth preserving. If what he says were true, it would have the effect of further embittering the afflicted people; as it was not true it was pernicious. He says they are scorned, yet suggests no compensation and makes no appeal in their behalf. There is not the least philanthropic intent. If it were an artistic study, or possessed any scientific interest, the absence of kindly purpose might be excused; but there is nothing in it worth an apology for its existence. Every attempt on his part to write a moral or draw a picture ends in the same way. He was absorbed in his books and the political excitements of his time, his vision only rested upon those who peopled his political experiences, and his mind comprehended closely, only what pertained to this domain.

As another instance of the same habit of defining qualities by circumstances which do not affect them, read his understanding of "A wise son rejoiceth his father, but a foolish son is a sorrow to his mother." He says, "The domestic joys and griefs of father and mother from their children are here distinguished, for a prudent and hopeful son is a capital pleasure to the father, who knows the value of virtue better than the mother, and therefore rejoices more at his son's disposition to virtue. This joy may also be heightened perhaps from seeing the good effect of his own management in the education of his son, so as to form good morals in him by precept and example. On the other hand, the mother suffers and partakes the most in the calamity of her son because the maternal affection is the more soft and tender, and again perhaps because she is conscious that her indulgence has spoiled and depraved him."

Bacon's faculty was for classification. His first thought was to assort the parts of a subject and label them. In his essays he proceeds upon this principle, arranging people in classes and ticketing them according to the properties peculiar to them. The following will be found among his observations :

"Old men are envious. Deformed people are all bold, malicious and, for the most, part, void of natural affection.

"Fathers know the value of virtue better than mothers, and rejoice in it more in their sons than do mothers. It is the father's management and example which forms the son's good morals. The mother's indulgence probably depraves the foolish son, and she feels the calamity more than the father.

"The errors of young men are the ruin of business, but the errors of old age amount to but this, that more could have been done and sooner.

"Young men in the conduct and management of actions embrace more than they can hold; stir more than they can quiet; fly to the end without consideration of the means and degrees; pursue some few principles which they have chanced upon absurdly; care not to innovate, which draws unknown inconveniences; use extreme remedies at first; and that, which doubleth all errors, will not acknowledge or retract them, like an unready horse, that will neither stop nor turn.

"Men of age object too much, consult too long, adventure too little, repent too soon, and seldom drive business home to the full period, but content themselves with a mediocrity of success.

"He that hath wife and children hath given hostages to fortune; for they are impediments to great enterprises, either of virtue or mischief.

"Certainly wife and children are a kind of discipline of humanity, and single men, though they be many times more charitable, because their means are less exhaust, yet, on the other side, they are more cruel and hard-hearted (good to make severe inquisitors), because their tenderness is not so often called upon. Grave natures, led by custom, and therefore constant, are commonly loving husbands."

"It is often seen that bad husbands have very good wives; whether it be that it raiseth the price of their husband's kindness when it comes, or that the wives take a pride in their patience; but this never fails, if the bad husbands were of their own choosing against their friends' consent, for then they will be sure to make good their folly.

"A man that hath no virtue in himself ever envieth virtue in others; for men's minds will either feed upon their own good or upon another's evil; and who wanteth the one will prey upon the other, and whoso is out of hope to attain another's virtue will seek to come at even hand, by depressing another's fortune.

"In the youth of a state arms do flourish, in the middle age of a state learning, and then both of them together for a time; in the declining age of a state mechanical arts and merchandise.

"Martial men are given to love as they are given to wine, for perils commonly ask to be paid in pleasures."

I have copied these extracts to show Bacon's habit of generalization. Yet some of his assertions are so singular that one wonders by what process of reasoning or by what experience he arrives at such conclusions.

It is unaccountable that young men should

be so rash and headstrong, "stir more than they can quiet, and fly to the end," etc., and yet not care to innovate.

If we accept his view, it never fails that when a woman takes a bad husband of her own free will and against the consent of her friends, she proves a patient wife and "makes good her folly."

If it is true that arts and manufactures flourish in the decline of a state, we have grave cause of alarm nowadays; and with such a view, why was it that he devoted so much study to this subject in the Novum Organum, and why did he attempt such a description of them in their perfection, in his ideal New Atlantis?

Perhaps it may be captious to ask these questions. The object is to urge simply that his writing is mostly of a hit-or-miss character; he was full of prejudices, and much that he wrote was dictated by the idea of the precept that he commends in his Essay on Ceremonies and Respects, viz., to "add something of one's own." If, in ordinary conversation, one should ramble on in such a chance fashion, lumping all people together and then dividing them up, in their mental qualities, affections and dispositions, by such arbitrary and accidental rules as age, sex and stature, he would either claim a large amount of indulgence or find few listeners. It is so directly the opposite of the poet, and particularly of Shakespeare, as to need scarcely a comment. In him there are no types, and not even two fools, alike. His is a faculty that has no rules, but is as free as the imagination; that reads intuitively the human mind and understands its motives, its reasonings, its humour, the impulses that govern its actions, its possibilities : the gift that creates individuals and peoples fiction with a world of characters as real as nature, as vivid as romance.

Bacon's mind is full of cures, of remedies and of recipes. He would construct and correct everything after some precept or prescription. He is so devoted to physics that he associates the qualities of the mind with the same nostrums that he would prescribe for the diseases of the body. He says of Friendship, "A principal fruit of friendship is the ease and discharge of the fulness and swellings of the heart, which passions of all kinds do cause and induce. We know diseases of stoppings and suffocations are the most dangerous of the body, and it is not much otherwise in the mind; you may take sarsaparilla to open the liver, steel to open the spleen, flour of sulphur for the lungs, castoream for the brain, but no receipt openeth the heart but a true friend."

This is a loathsome simile of a beautiful human quality, and his conception of the quality was on a level with his gross description of it. Such extracts from Bacon must constantly challenge comparison between his inelegant, mechanical writing and the chaste and dainty work of the plays.

He would have made poets to order after a scientific method. He says, "Histories make men wise; poets, witty; the mathematics, subtle; natural philosophy, deep, moral, grave; logic and rhetoric, able to contend; studies become habits; nay, there is no stand or impediment in the wit, but may be wrought out by fit studies, like as diseases of the body may have appropriate exercises; bowling is good for the stone and reins, shooting for the lungs and breast, gentle walking for the stomach, riding for the head, and the like; so, if a man's wits be wandering, let him study the mathematics; for in demonstration, if his wit be called away never so little, he must begin again ; if his wit be not apt to distinguish or find differences, let him study the schoolmen, for they are 'splitters of hairs.' If he be not apt to beat over matters and to call up one thing to prove and illustrate another, let him study lawyers' cases ; so every defect of the mind may have a special receipt."

Those who think Shakespeare could not have written the plays because he had no great school learning ought to be in love with Bacon's idea of tinkering the human mind, of patching up its defects and doctoring its ailments ; for the probability of his having written the plays, in their judgment, rests entirely upon his erudition. They credit him with the poetic gift upon the same ground that he professes to be able to manufacture it.

Upon the same theory an artist might be fashioned, or a composer, or a genius of any kind. You must simply discover what he lacks, and as "there is no stand or impediment that may not be wrought out by fit studies," it becomes only a question of what peculiar kind of cramming the defective poet needs.

After reading such compositions as these extracts from Bacon's essays, it is impossible to imagine their author constantly fired by an uncontrollable desire to steal away from such "serious observations," to some secret corner, to dash off one of Shakespeare's plays, in foolhardy risk of his reputation. It must be remembered that these essays were written by one who is considered by his admirers, the most learned of his day. If some aged and discoloured college archives could be discovered to show that Shakespeare had passed a few terms in classic studies, it might be a satisfaction to those who cannot believe in his authorship because they do not know where he learned to read, but with these essays in evidence that would be their only value. The beauty of Shakespeare's creations is their simplicity, naturalness and originality, features which, by the testimony of the "Essays," such studies might have dimned, but could not have brightened.

In the introduction to Bacon's Essays by Mr. Joseph Devey, M.A., he says, "To rid himself (Bacon) of embarrassment so irksome to men of genius, he resolved to make a bold attempt to retrieve his affairs by marriage. Lady Hatton, the eldest daughter of Sir Thomas Cecil, and early relict of the son of Chancellor Hatton, was the beauty at whose shrine Bacon ventured to offer up his first vows. (Macaulay says, 'The eccentric manner and violent temper of this woman made her a disgrace and torment to her connections.') But the rich widow had unfortunately possessed herself of a copy of Bacon's Essays, and finding therein love described as an ignoble passion, fit only for base and petulant natures, she ascribed his professions of attachment rather to her money than her person, and rejected his suit. The disappointment was the more severely felt, as the young lady capitulated to a rival, his own antagonist, Sir Edward Coke, a crabbed old lawyer with six children and stricken with infirmities."

BACON'S ESSAY ON LOVE.

"The stage is more beholding to love than the life of man; for as to the stage, love is ever a matter of comedies and now and then of tragedies, but in life it doth much mischief, sometimes like a siren, sometimes like a fury. You may observe that amongst all the great and worthy persons (whereof the memory remaineth either ancient or recent) there is not one that has been transported to the mad degree of love, which shows that great spirits and great business do keep out this weak passion. You must except, nevertheless, Marcus Antonius, the half-partner of the empire of Rome, and Appius Claudius, the decemvir and lawgiver, whereof the former was indeed a voluptuous man and inordinate, but the latter was an austere and wise man; and therefore it seems (though rarely) that love can find entrance, not only into an open heart, but also into a heart well fortified, if watch be not well kept. It is a poor saying of Epicurus, 'We are a sufficient theme of contemplation, the one for the other,' as if a man made for the contemplation of the heavens and all noble objects, should do nothing but kneel before a little idol and make himself subject, though not of the mouth (as beasts are), yet of the eye, which was given him for higher purposes. It is a strange thing to note the excess of this passion and how it braves the nature and value of things by this, that the speaking in hyperbole is comely in nothing but in love, neither is it merely in the phrase; for whereas it hath been well said, 'That the arch flatterer, with whom all the petty flatterers have intelligence, is a man's self,' certainly the lover is more; for there never was a proud man thought so absurdly well of himself, as the lover doth of the person loved, and therefore it was well said, 'That it is impossible to love and be wise.' Neither doth this weakness appear to others only and not to the party loved, but the loved one most of all, except the love be reciprocal, for it is a true rule that love is ever rewarded either with the reciprocal, or with an inward and secret contempt; by how much the more men ought to beware of this passion, which loseth not only other things, but itself. As for the other losses, the poet's relation doth well figure them: 'That he that preferred Helena, quitted the gifts of Juno and Pallas; for whosoever esteemeth too much of amorous affection, quitteth both riches and wisdom. This passion hath its floods in the very times of weakness, which are great prosperity and great adversity, though this latter hath been less observed, both which tonics kindle love and make it more fervent, and therefore show it to be the child of folly. They do best, who, if they cannot but admit love, yet make it keep quarter, and sever it wholly from their serious affairs and actions of life; for if it check once with business, it troubleth men's fortunes, and maketh men that they can nowise be true to their own ends. I know not how, but martial men are given to love; I think it is but as they are given to wine, for perils commonly ask to be paid in pleasures. There is in man's nature a secret inclination and motion towards love of others, which, if it be not spent upon some one or a few, doth naturally spread itself towards many, and maketh men become humane and charitable, as is seen sometimes in friars. Nuptial love maketh mankind, friendly love perfecteth it, but wanton love corrupteth and embaseth it."

Bacon afterwards married a rich alderman's daughter, who probably had not read his sentiments on the "child of folly." In order to help his suit he petitioned Cecil that he might be knighted, which was done along with a batch of about three hundred others. He had no children, and his wife was divorced after his disgrace.

I imagine not many people will need more

than to read his Essay on Love, to dismiss any thought of his having written any of Shakespeare's plays, where "the lover thinks so absurdly well of the party loved."

It is said that "all the world is in love with a lover," but Bacon is an exception. He is much vexed with a lover. To him love is a fury, or a siren, and does much mischief. It is of more service to comedy than to life. It is a weakness. Only two great persons are known to have been transported to its "mad degree." Great persons and great business do not allow it entrance. It is altogether beneath the dignity of great and worthy men, who were made to contemplate the heavens, to kneel before a little idol and make themselves subjects of the eye, which was given them for higher purposes. Shakespeare had no thought of that kind, and his plays are full of the little idols who are perfectly bewitched by the eyes of mortals, who never seem to suspect that they were intended purely for astronomical study.

> "Tell me, where is fancy bred,
> Or in the heart, or in the head?
> How begot, how nourished?
> Reply, reply,

> It is engendered in the eyes,
> With gazing fed ; and fancy dies
> In the cradle where it lies.
>   Let us all ring fancy's knell ;
>   I'll begin it,—Ding, dong, bell."
> —*Merchant of Venice.*

> "Her eye discourses ; I will answer it.
> I am too bold, 'tis not to me she speaks ;
> Two of the fairest stars in all the heaven,
> Having some business, do entreat her eyes
> To twinkle in the spheres till they return.
> What if her eyes were there, they in her head?
> The brightness of her cheek would shame those stars,
> As daylight doth a lamp ; her eye in heaven
> Would through the airy region stream so bright,
> That birds would sing, and think it were not night."
> —*Romeo and Juliet.*

> "Her eyes, like marigolds, had sheathed their light,
> And, canopied in darkness, sweetly lay
> Till they might open to adorn the day."—*Lucrece.*

The Midsummer Night's Dream, in utter disregard of Bacon's disapproval, makes the whole plot of the story turn upon the witchery of the fairy's touch to mortal eyes.

> "*Oberon.*—And with the juice of this I'll streak her eyes,
>   And make her full of hateful fantasies."

> "*Oberon.*—What thou seest when thou dost wake,
>   Do it for thy true love take :
>   Love, and languish for his sake ;
>   Be it ounce, or cat, or bear,

> Pard, or boar with bristled hair,
> In thy eye that shall appear
> When thou wak'st, it is thy dear;
> Wake when some vile thing is near."
>
> "*Puck.*—Through the forest I have gone,
> But Athenian found I none,
> On whose eyes I might approve
> This flower's force in stirring love.
> Night and silence— Who is here?
> Weeds of Athens he doth wear;
> This is he, my master said,
> Despised the Athenian maid;
> And here the maiden, sleeping sound,
> On the dank and dirty ground.
> Pretty soul, she durst not lie
> Near this lack-love, kill-courtesy.
> Churl, upon thy eyes I throw
> All the power this charm doth owe.
> When thou wak'st, let love forbid
> Sleep his seat on thy eyelid;
> So awake when I am gone,
> For I must now to Oberon."

This does not suggest any of the dangerous things that may befall those who admit love. It even sounds as though the one thing that mortals most delight in, were that which they cannot have and "be wise."

There perhaps never was a lover who thought as "absurdly well" of the "*party* loved" as Romeo. Imagine Juliet as a "party"! Bacon could never have had any patience with such folly as Romeo's hyperbole. Carlyle said that "Bacon could no more have written Hamlet than he could have made this planet." It is even more impossible to imagine him as the author of Midsummer Night's Dream and Romeo and Juliet.

A man who could see nothing but "childish" curiosity in the figures of a dance, who considered love the "child of folly," and "works of imagination" a culpable loss of time, must sit like a bat at such a spectacle as the Midsummer Night's Dream.

Bacon's admirers must assume that his Essay on Love was a jest, or admit that he could not have contained, much less depicted, the spirit and enjoyment of the Midsummer Night's Dream, Romeo and Juliet, or any play or romance where love, or humour, is the theme. His sphynx-like, impassive survey of the tender passion, is incompatible with the fancy to delineate either such an ardent devotee as Romeo, or such a dissolute deceiver as Falstaff. Had he been gifted with such power, the Queen's command for a repeated presentation of the fat knight, offered him the golden opportunity to realise the wish closest to his heart: her recognition of his merit.

In whatever he has written, whatever business of life he was engaged upon, there is no hint, suggestion, or act, to excite even a suspicion of such thoughts as abound in the elfish dreamland scenes of the Midsummer Night, the mirth and burlesque of the Merry Wives, or the pathetic misfortunes of Ophelia and Desdemona. His Essay on Cupid offers a parallel of comparison, in some respects more noteworthy than his Essay on Love. He entitles it :

"CUPID OR ATOM, EXPLAINED OF THE CORPUSCULAR PHILOSOPHY.

"Love seems to be the appetite or incentive of the primitive matter; or, to speak more distinctly, the natural motion or moving principle of the original corpuscles or atoms, this being the most ancient and only power that made and wrought all things out of matter.

"Cupid is elegantly drawn as a perpetual child, for compounds are larger things, and have their periods of age; but the first seeds or atoms of bodies are small, and remain in perpetual infant state.

"He is again justly represented naked; as all compounds may properly be said to be dressed and clothed, or to assume a personage, whence nothing remains truly naked but the original particle of things.

"The last attribute of Cupid is archery, viz., a virtue or power of operating at a distance, for everything that operates at a distance may seem, as it were, to dart or shoot with arrows. And whoever allows of atoms and vacuity, necessarily supposes that the virtue of atoms operates at a distance ; for without this operation no motion could be excited, on account of the vacuum interposing, but all things would remain sluggish and unmoved."

As Shakespeare had not Bacon's learning, it may be assumed that he did not know of the corpuscular nature of Puck, nor that he was not a compound, but fortunately was a particle of things, otherwise he would have been obliged to wear clothes. It is fortunate also that he did not know of the dangers that beset Puck in the shape of the "vacuum interposing," which might in some blundering way have made Puck sluggish and bedraggled him, so to speak.

Bacon's essay on the scientific origin of Cupid and Shakespeare's personification of

Cupid, are as fair examples of the difference in the natures of the two men as can be drawn. The more one learns of Bacon's attainments, his study and investigation, the better satisfied one becomes that Shakespeare was without them. What a misfortune it would have been for Shakespeare to have had his fancy clouded by a knowledge that the little sprite was a corpuscle, and that some atmospheric calamity might befall him that would instantly render him torpid!

We can find something of the idea of Puck—

"I'll put a girdle round about the earth
In forty minutes,"

in Bacon, but it is not expressed in the same way. He is speaking "drawingly" of hope, as nearly as can be made out, and says, "Nor should we neglect to mention the prophecy of Daniel, of the last days of the world, 'Many shall run to and fro, and knowledge shall be increased,' thus plainly hinting and suggesting that fate (which is providence) would cause the complete circuit of the globe (now accomplished or at least going forward by means of so many distant voyages) and the increase of learning to happen at the same epoch." This is not exactly as Puck expresses it, but it is absolute collusion compared with some instances cited in support of the Baconite theory.

The charm of all the elfish world is its unreality. Bacon would destroy all of that and account for its existence upon scientific principles. He would never be satisfied with a Cupid that he could not dissect. In nothing else is he so far from Shakespeare as in Shakespeare's fairyland. These airy visions cannot find any place in the material of his philosophy. The truant and intangible nature of the shadowy creatures, could never dwell in the atmosphere of his corpuscles. The man who can speak of Cupid as "the appetite or incentive of the primitive matter" could not follow him through the Midsummer Night's Dream. It is not the kind of a play that a man would write who took a scientific or anatomical view of Cupid, or who regarded love as the "child of folly," or whose description of love would frighten away his sweetheart.

Bacon is the only poet in history who despises love, and the only one whose love-song scared away a fortune and a wife.

CHAPTER VI.

The New Atlantis—Bacon's sketch of Queen Elizabeth—His censure of fictions of the imagination—His resolve to publish all his writings—Time occupied in writing the plays—The Sonnets—Queen Elizabeth's dislike to Bacon—His propensity to borrow—His lack of traits that are glorified by Shakespeare.

THE only thing that I have found in Bacon's works which approaches a sketch of an imaginary female character, is in the New Atlantis, and she is out of sight, in a loft, and does not say anything. The New Atlantis is, I think, his only attempt at fiction. He did not finish it! Rawley says, "His desire of collecting the natural history diverted him, which he preferred many degrees before it." It is scarcely necessary to say it is not a love story. The distinguishing characteristic of the hero is a large family and great wisdom, but, as "wise men never admit love lest it may trouble their fortunes and make them that they can in nowise be true to their own ends," these clashing elements do not disturb the solemnity of Bacon's romance; "as for masculine love they have no touch of it." The story is a grave and serious study. It opens about twenty years after the ascension, with a miracle that proves to be a floating column of light. It is far out at sea, and the eddies set off from it in every direction, so that boats cannot approach, until one of the faithful in one of the boats which has been paddled out to investigate the illumination, bethinks himself to make a "confession of faith that the thing which we now see before us is a true miracle." Then, that one boat is no longer repelled from the marvellous sight, but is unbound and suffers itself to be rowed toward it, whereupon this immense structure, some miles high, with a resplendent cross upon it, explodes into a firmament of stars and disappears, leaving only a little ark floating close at hand, which upon being taken in tow is found to contain a letter and a volume embracing all the canonical books, and the first copies of some other books which (the author admits) were not written at that time; in fact, not until some centuries later.

The letter explains the books, and has miraculous power. Hebrews, Persians and Indians can read it alike as if printed in their own language; and "thus the land was saved from infidelity. Thereafter none but Christians were allowed to land upon the island where these people dwelt."

There is no other form of narrative so cheap and unimaginative as the miraculous. It hesitates at no degree of improbability. It sets all natural laws and human experience at defiance. Absurdity is not an obstacle, and originality not a requisite. If one has not invention to plan the opening of a story, or a reasonable ground for a theory, he can begin with a dream, or an apparition, or a column of light or some astronomical freak, and get his tale launched in that way; but it denotes a dearth of imagination and is barren of originality. He simply needs to talk about it in an awestruck and sanctimonious way; and though he may be of the slipperiest clay himself, his supposed faith in the supernatural will be accepted for spirituality. The common-place accessories of all such accounts destroy the intended effect.

The Mormon birth, resuscitation, or excavation, of their theology, shows to what extent people will attempt to join the material with the spiritual. The Mormons claim that the plates from which the Book of Mormon was printed were delivered to Mr. Joseph Smith, Jr., by an angel, September 22, 1827, in the woods in New York state, where they had been buried fourteen hundred years. A key was also there, to explain the plates, described in this way : " With the records was found a curious instrument, called by the ancients the Urim and Thummim, which consisted of two transparent stones, clear as crystal, set in two rims of bow. This was used in ancient times by people called seers. It was an instrument by the use of which they received revelation of things past or future." Then, after Mr. Joseph Smith, Jr., received the plates, he had considerable trouble to remove them, for this Mormon angel seems to have felt no further responsibility about them ; and Mr. Smith finally carted them away *concealed in a barrel of beans*, being overhauled by constables with search-warrants, and pursued by ruffians with shot-guns and clubs. That is all set forth with about the same solemnity as Bacon's birth of the community of Solomon's House.

The plot or plan of the New Atlantis seems

to be an enumeration of the things *we have.* The one thing which he mentions that we *have not,* is masculine love, and the absence of that is regarded as one of the community's blessings. Among the things specified which "we have" are "all sorts of beasts and birds which we use for dissection and trials, wherein we find many strange effects; as continuing life in them though divers parts, which others account vital, be perished and taken forth; resuscitating of some that seem dead in appearance, and the like. We try poisons and other medicines upon them, as well of surgery as physic. We dwarf them. We make a number of serpents, worms, flies, fishes, of putrefaction, etc. [Some of the diversions of these ideal people are too disgusting to copy.] We try experiments in burying some in one kind of earth, some in another, some in water. We also generate bodies in the air, as frogs, flies and divers others."

This story of the New Atlantis is simply an existence where the people have everything that the author conceives to be desirable. There is no theatre! There are no plays! The only poetry they have is that which praises

Adam, Noah and Abraham, **solely because they were the fathers of mankind.** Shakespeare would have had no occupation there. I doubt if he would have been permitted to land, and I am convinced he would not have wished to.

This is the description of the entry of one of the fathers of Solomon's House: "The day being come, he made his entry. He was a man of middle stature and age, comely of person, and had an aspect as if he pitied men. He was clothed in a robe of fine black cloth, with wide sleeves and a cape. His undergarment was of excellent white linen down to the foot, girt with a girdle of the same; and a sindon or tippet of the same about his neck. He had gloves that were canvas and set with stone, and shoes of peach-coloured velvet. His neck was bare to the shoulders. His hat was like a helmet or Spanish montera, and his locks curled below it decently. They were of colour brown. His beard was cut round, and of the same colour with his hair, somewhat lighter. He was carried in a rich chariot, without wheels, litter-wise, with two horses at each end, richly trapped in blue velvet embroidered, and two footmen on either side in the like attire. The chariot was all of cedar, gilt, and adorned with crystal, save that the fore end had panels of sapphires set in borders of gold, and the hinder end the like of emeralds of the Peru colour. There was also a sun of gold, radiant upon the top, in the midst; and on the top before a small cherub of gold, with wings displayed. The chariot was covered with cloth of gold tissued upon blue. He had before him fifty attendants, young men all, in white satin loose coats up to the middle leg, and stocking of white silk, and shoes of blue velvet, and hats of blue velvet, with fine plumes of divers colours set round like hat bands. Next before the chariot went two men bareheaded, in linen garments down to the foot, girt, and shoes of blue velvet, who carried, the one a crosier, the other a pastoral staff, like a sheephook, neither of them of metal, but the crosier of balmwood, the pastoral staff of cedar. Horsemen he had none, neither before nor behind his chariot, as it seemeth to avoid all tumult and trouble. Behind his chariot went all the officers and principals of the companies of the city. He sat alone upon cushions of a kind of excellent plush, blue, and under his foot curious carpets of silk of divers colours, like the Persian, but far finer. He held up his bare hand as he went, as blessing the people, but in silence. The street was wonderfully well kept, so that there never was any army had their men stand in better battle array than the people stood. The windows likewise were not crowded, but every one stood in them as if they had been placed."

This is a description of the stately entrance of one of the wise men of this ideal community. It gives Bacon's highest conception of what constitutes an imposing pageant and the homage of the people to one of their rulers. Whether there is anything Shakespearean in the description or in the spirit of the ceremony is a matter of individual judgment. It does not capture the fancy to imagine this dignitary "with an aspect as though he pitied men," with his bare neck and shoulders and his hair curling decently beneath his helmet, shod in peach-coloured shoes, resting on "carpet like Persian, only far finer," or that the "fore end" of the chariot had panels of one kind and the "hinder end, the like of emeralds of the Peru colour."

A bumpkin describing a Lord Mayor's Show

could not use more commonplace terms or more homely similes. He describes, to quote from his Essay on Masques, "the things which catch the sense." In everything, the absence of the sentimental, and the dominant sway of the material, is conspicuous. His theme, in this description of a perfect house, is the creature comforts, the conveniences and personal requisites that the people enjoy. He fills pages with catalogues of these.

"We have towers half a mile high on mountains, that raise them at least three miles high. We use them for isolation, refrigeration, conservation. We use them to observe fiery meteors, etc., and we have hermits dwelling there whom we instruct what to observe.

"We have great fresh lakes and salt lakes, fish-fowl cataracts, which serve for motors, also engines.

"We have artificial wells, fountains, tincted upon vitriol, sulphur, steel, brass, lead, nitre and other minerals; wells for infusions such as 'water of paradise' for the prolongation of life. We have spacious houses to imitate thunder, lightning, meteors, snow and hail.

"We have chambers of health for the cure of diseases, and baths for the same purpose.

"We have orchards, gardens, trees, herbs, berries, 'all kinds of drinks,' besides vineyards, grafting, inoculation, wild trees and fruit trees. Their fruit is larger and sweeter than its nature, its smell, taste and colour is superior, and it has medicinal uses.

"We raise plants without seeds, and we can turn one plant or tree into another. We have parks and enclosures for beasts and birds, upon which we practice vivisection. We have pools for fishes for the purpose of like experiments.

"We have brew-houses, bake-houses and kitchens, divers drinks, breads and meats, rare and of special effects. Wines of grapes, and drinks of other juice, of fruits, of grains, and of roots, and of mixtures with honey, sugar and manna, and fruits dried and decocted, also of tears, or woundings of trees, and of the pulp of canes, and these drinks are of several ages, some to the age or last of at least forty years.

"We have drinks also brewed with several herbs and roots and spices, yea, with several fleshes, and white meats; whereof some of the drinks are such, as they are in effect meat and drink both, so that divers, especially in age, do desire to live with them, with little or no meat or bread. And above all, we strive to have drinks of extreme thin parts, to insinuate into the body and yet without all biting, sharpness or fretting; insomuch as some of them put upon the back of your hand will, with a little stay, pass through to the palm, and yet taste mild to the mouth. We also ripen waters until they become nourishing.

"Breads we have of several grains, roots and kernels; yea, and some of flesh and fish dried, with divers kinds of leavenings and seasonings. So for meats, we have some of them so beaten and made tender and mortified, yet without all corrupting, as a weak heat of the stomach will turn them into good chylus.

"We have dispensatories or shops of medicine, and drugs in immense variety. We have distillations, preparations, separations and percolations.

"We have papers, linens, silks, tissues, feathers and dyes.

"We have fertilizers [too offensive to describe.] We have furnaces, magnifying-glasses, loadstones.

"We have echo-houses, musical instruments, bells, gunpowder, fireworks."

If the best marketing, the finest and most suitable clothing, perfect sanitary plumbing, mineral baths, all kinds of drinks, medicines drugs, and vivisection as a scientific pastime, can make people happy, then Bacon has described Utopia; but not in the phrase that Shakespeare would have devoted to a theme so lofty and prolific. Bacon's frequent recurrence to drink, in this wonderful picture of mortal bliss, suggests a comparison between the terms he uses and the prose Shakespeare puts into the mouth of Falstaff, in relishing of the same topic.

"A good sherris sack hath a two-fold operation in it. It ascends me into the brain; dries me there all the foolish, and dull, and crudy vapours which environ it; makes it apprehensive, quick, forgetive, full of nimble, fiery and delectable shapes; which deliver'd o'er to the voice, (the tongue) which is the birth, becomes excellent wit. The second property of your excellent sherris is the warming of the blood: which, before cold and settled, left the liver white and pale, which is the badge of pussilanimity and cowardice; but the sherris warms it, and makes it course from the inwards to the parts extreme ; it illumineth the face which, as a beacon, gives warning to all the rest of this little kingdom, man, to arm ; and then the vital commoners, and inland petty spirits, muster me all to their captain, the heart, who great and puffed up with this retinue, doth any deed of courage ; and this valour comes of sherris."

But, to return to Bacon's idea of the perfect sphere ; lest it may appear that the people have no amusements other than trying poisons upon the brute creation, I will copy the description of the feast which they celebrate. This feast is one of the principal features of the romance. It reads : "One day there were two of our company bidden to a feast of the family, as they call it, a most natural, pious and reverend custom it is, showing that nation to be compounded of all goodness. This is the manner of it : it is granted to any man, that shall live to see thirty persons, descended of his body, alive together and all above three years old, to make this feast, which is done at the cost of the state. The father of the family, whom they call the tirsan, two days before the feast taketh to him three of such friends as he liketh to choose, and is assisted also by the governor of the city or place where the feast is celebrated, and all the persons of the family of both sexes are summoned to attend him. These two days the tirsan sitteth in consultation concerning the good estate of the family. There, if there be any discord or suits between any of the family, they are compounded and appeased; there, if any of the family be distressed or decayed, order is taken for their relief and competent means to live; there, if any be subject to vice or to take ill courses, they are reproved and censured. So likewise direction is given touching marriage and the course of life which any of them should take, with divers other the like orders and advices. The governor assisteth to the end to put in execution by his public authority the decrees and orders of the tirsan, if they should be disobeyed, though that seldom needeth, such reverence and obedience they give to the order of nature. The tirsan doth then ever choose one man from amongst his sons to live in house with him, who is called ever after 'the son of the vine.' The reason will hereafter appear. On the feast day the father or tirsan cometh forth after divine service into a large room where the feast is celebrated, which room hath a half-pace (platform) at the upper end. Against the wall in the middle of the platform is a chair placed for him with a table and a carpet before it. Over the chair is a state made round or oval, and it is of ivy somewhat whiter than ours. . . .

"The tirsan cometh forth with all his generation or lineage, the males before him and the females following him.

"And if there be a mother from whose body the whole lineage is descended, there is a traverse placed in a loft above on the right hand of the chair, with a private door, and a carved window of glass, leaded with gold and blue, where she sitteth but is not seen.

"When the tirsan is come forth, he sitteth down in the chair, and all the lineage place themselves against the wall, both at his back and upon the sides of the platform, in order of their years, without difference of sex, and stand upon their feet. When he is set, the room being always full of company, but well kept, and without disorder, after some pause there cometh in from the lower end of the room a taratan, which is as much as an herald, and on either side of him two young lads, whereof one carrieth a scroll of their shining yellow parchment, and the other a cluster of grapes of gold, with a long foot or stalk; the herald and children are clothed with mantles of sea-water green satin, but the herald's mantle is streamed with gold and hath a train. Then the herald with three courtesies, or rather inclinations, cometh up as far as the platform and there first taketh into his hand the scroll.

"This scroll is the king's charter, containing gift of revenue, and many privileges, exemptions and points of honour granted to the father of the family; and it is ever styled and directed to such an one, our well-beloved friend and creditor, which is a proper title only in this case; for they say, the king is debtor to no man, but for propagation of his subjects. The seal set to the king's charter is the king's image, embossed or mounted in gold. This charter the herald readeth aloud, and while it is read, the father or tirsan standeth up, supported by two of his sons, such as he chooseth. Then the herald mounteth the platform and delivereth the charter into his hand, at which there is an acclamation, by all that are present, in their language, which is thus much: Happy are the people of Bensalem. Then the herald taketh into his hand from the other child the cluster of grapes which is of gold, both the stalk and the grapes, but the grapes are daintily enamelled; and if the males of the family be the greater number, the grapes are enamelled purple, with a little sun set on the top; if the females, then they are enamelled with a greenish yellow, with a crescent on the top. The grapes are in number as many as there are descendants of the family. This golden cluster the herald delivereth also to the tirsan, who presently delivereth it over to that son that he had formerly chosen to be in house with him, who beareth it before his father as an ensign of honour when he goeth in public ever after; and is thereupon called the son of the vine.

"After this ceremony ended, the father or tirsan retireth, and after some time cometh forth again to dinner, where he sitteth alone under the state as before, and none of his descendants sit with him of what degree or dignity soever, except he be of Solomon's House.

"He is served only by his own children such as are male, who perform to him all service of the table upon the knee, and all the women only stand about him, leaning against the wall. The room below his platform hath tables on the sides for the guests that are bidden, who are served with great and comely order; and toward the end of the dinner, which in the greatest feasts with them lasteth never more than an hour and a half, there is a hymn sung, varied according to the invention of him that composed it, for they have excellent poetry, but the subject of it is always the praise of Adam and Noah and Abraham, whereof the former two peopled the world, and the last was the father of the faithful.

"Dinner being done the tirsan retireth again, and having withdrawn himself alone into a place where he maketh some private prayers, he cometh forth the third time to give the blessing with all his descendants about him as at the first.

"Then the tirsan blesses each one individually with a set phrase—'Son or daughter of Bensalem, thy father saith it, the man by whom thou hast breath and life speaketh the word. Sons, it is well with you that you are born,' etc."

It is reasonable to suppose that Bacon in imagination performed the part of tirsan. It describes a scene and a figure suited to his ambition and aspiration. He had an overpowering desire to be wise, or to be so regarded, and his fancy always leans to the grave and venerable. This story is told simply as a picture of Bacon's conception of an ideal existence.

I have read praises of this paper, but I can only see in it the unctuous vulgarity of a nature fond of show, ceremony, parade, homage and incense ; and barren of sentiment, poetry, grace and spirituality.

There is not the slightest evidence that this feast "shows the state to be compounded of all goodness ;" in fact it is not a feast at all, but only *a feed for the old tirsan*, and the occasion of it is too vulgar to be hidden by the pretence of religious fervour. Such a ceremony could only be imagined by a man of earthy tastes who was fond of picturing himself the object of adulation, awe and worship. It could have no other purpose. If one can forget its selfishness and its disgusting features, it may become amusing, but it has nothing in it worthy of serious thought, evoking any rapture, or displaying in the least the genial power and fanciful moods of the great poet.

It could not be enjoyable to any one but the old tirsan, and only one who expected to play the tirsan would have written it; it is the most unjust to the woman who is stuck away in the loft. As the party is the reward for the successful rearing of a numerous offspring, one naturally resents the banishment of the member of the family whose claims to recognition must be immensely greater than those of the old tirsan. It is a very modest meal for a state to set forth which has such abundance of every conceivable thing to eat and drink; and the neighbours seem to partake in a stealthy and timid way at the side tables only, while the lineage do not appear to get any of the refreshments at all. *They* do not even have seats. In fact, the company seems to be invited to see the host eat. It may be that the progeny of this old man are stupid enough to be lost in admiration of their progenitor, but it is more likely that they regard him as a curiosity, and that only the presence of the policeman (governor) restrains them from poking fun at him. Some of them may be dull enough to enjoy the spectacle of "him from whom they have life and breath" sitting at a table alone, with his back to them, taking his food, served by his sons on their knees; but the "decayed" ones must with "hearts distrusting, ask if this be joy," and the little three-year-old tots—by nature always hungry—down at the far end of the line, can hardly be expected to appreciate the nature of the celebration, or to look with any great degree of satisfaction or patience, upon the morsels that disappear at the solitary repast; I should think they might be sadly in need of the mother's care, who is secreted above where she may peep through an opening to see the father of her children get his diploma and gorge himself for ninety minutes.

She is treated as though in disgrace, she gets none of the viands, and does not mingle with the company. If she is the mother of the *whole thirty*, she may sit in this concealment and spy at her sons holding up their aged father, while the herald reads the charter; she may see the family line ranged along the wall "in the order of their years," and she may see her sons ply the old man with the food that the state has provided; but, if some other mother may have contributed a share of the thirty pledges, there seems to be no provision for her whatever, and the presumption is that she could not even have a hiding-place, to peep at what is going on. If she were a widow and the lineage fulfilled the requirement of the ordinance, were she ever so needy, the state could not provide the feast; for it is an honour and a debt that the state pays only to the tirsan.

If there is anything in this story that suggests the writer of Shakespeare's plays, then I have aided the Baconite theory in making such lengthy extracts from it. It is Bacon's one venture in the realm of narrative, and it is not wonderful that he had not sufficient fondness for the subject to finish it. "He preferred natural history many degrees," but it is so much like his Natural History that one can hardly realize his distaste for it on that ground. If a story that contains a laboratory, dissecting-room, dye-houses, observatories, and in which they manufacture thunder, lightning and com-posts, and generate frogs, flies and worms, and in which all the affairs are conducted upon scientific principles, does not satisfy a would-be scientist's longing in such respects, what must be thought of an attempt to attribute to him such works as the Midsummer Night's Dream,

Comedy of Errors, Much Ado about Nothing, or the Merry Wives of Windsor?

Lest some readers may think Bacon had some intention of adding amusement to this story, and that there was a possibility of the "child of folly" finally getting entrance, I may say that the part yet to be added was the legal department. His historians say he intended to frame a code of laws for Solomon's House. If the treatment of the mother of the tirsan's children and a law they had respecting marriage are to speak for him as a law-giver, then the world has lost nothing by the unfinished construction of Solomon's House. This law reads thus: "Marriage without consent of parents they do not make void, but they mulct it in the inheritors, for the children of such marriages are not admitted to inherit above a third part of their parents' inheritance."

The same disposition to see only the gross and material side of his subject appears in all his writings. Even in his history of Queen Elizabeth, instead of a description of her wit, tastes, habits, disposition and personal appearance, and such things as have a living interest for the mass of people, his chief stress is laid upon her sickness. "In the distemper of the queen there was nothing shocking, nothing presaging, nothing unbecoming of human nature. She was not desirous of life, nor impatient under sickness, nor racked with pain. She had no dire or disagreeable symptom, but all things were of that kind as argued rather the frailty than the corruption or disgrace of nature. Being emaciated by an extreme dryness of body and the cares that attend a crown, and never refreshed with wine or with a full and plentiful diet, she was a few days before her death struck with a dead palsy."

The peculiarities and characteristics of the queen who boxed her courtier's ears, and danced measures and galliards for her Italian guest when she was nearly seventy, to show that she was not as old as people would have her, and who "danced so high and composedly," did not interest him, and his sketch was chiefly a diagnosis of her.

The time that Bacon would have required for writing the plays seems to have received very little attention from his admirers. It is admitted even by them that no tangible evidence of his authorship exists. His historians say he was constantly attended by a chaplain and a secretary. It would have been an impossible task to do such an amount of work and conceal all traces and evidences of it from persons so closely connected with him, especially considering the care bestowed upon his manuscripts and the care with which they were preserved.

Bacon "entered upon the study of the law when he was twenty, and rarely suffered either amusement or literature to disturb the tenor of his professional duties for ten or eleven years" (Devey). This brings him to 1591 ; and from that time forth his life was in full public view.

He felicitates himself, in his Novum Organum, on the amount of work he has done under disadvantages, and holds himself up as an example to others in this respect; and not only does not refer to any other writing, but gives a side thrust at learning that is not "sound;" the same censure that he applied to stage acting in his essays. He says, Book I., Aphorism CXI., "Nor should we omit to mention another ground of hope. Let men only consider (if they will) their infinite expenditure of talent, time and fortune, in matters and studies of far inferior importance and value; a small proportion of which applied to sound and solid learning, would be sufficient to overcome every difficulty. And we have thought right to add this observation, because we candidly own that such a collection of natural and experimental history as we have traced in our mind, and as really necessary, is a great and as it were royal work, requiring much labour and expense."

CXII. "The particular phenomena of the arts and nature are in reality but as a handful when compared with the *fictions of the imagination, removed and separated from the evidence of facts.* The termination of our method is clear, and as I had almost said, near at hand; *the other admits of no termination, but only of infinite confusion.* For men have hitherto dwelt but little or rather only slightly touched upon experience, whilst *they have wasted much time on theories and the fictions of the imagination."* (The italics are mine.)

CXIII. "We think some ground of hope is afforded by our own example, which is not mentioned for the sake of boasting, but as a useful remark. Let those who distrust their own powers observe myself, one who have amongst my contemporaries been the most engaged in public business, who am not very strong in health (which causes a great loss of time), and am the first explorer of this course, following the guidance of none, nor even communicating my thoughts to a single individual; yet having once firmly entered in the right way, and submitting the powers of my mind to things, I have somewhat advanced (as I make bold to think) that matter I now treat of. Then let others consider what may be hoped from men who enjoy abundant leisure, from united labours," etc.

CXVI. "We offer no universal or complete theory. The time does not yet appear to us to have arrived, and we entertain no hope of our life being prolonged to the completion to the sixth part of the Instauration," etc.

Bacon's earnestness in that work is undeniable, whatever the ambition may have been. The tone and phraseology is straitforward and unlike the affectation and pedantry of his essays. He speaks here of his Novum Organum as solid and sound learning, and deprecates the time, talent and fortune that "people waste upon studies of *far inferior value and im-*

portance, viz., *works of fiction and the imagination, which admit of no termination and only of confusion."* In order to encourage others he reminds them of how much he has done himself, although engrossed in public business and having lost much time from delicate health, and he fears he may not live to finish a part of his work "which is destined for philosophy discovered by the interpretation of nature."

In another place he says, "I determined to publish whatever I found time to perfect. Nor is this the haste of ambition, but anxiety that if I should die there might remain behind me some outline and determination of the matter my mind has embraced," etc.

This sentence, written by himself, that he determined to publish whatever he had time to perfect, sounds much like an unconscious disclaimer to any title to the Shakespeare plays.

As Ben Jonson, Herbert and Playfair assisted Bacon in his translations, it is quite probable that Bacon's regrets at the time, talent and money wasted on works of fiction and imagination were directed at them.

Bacon's metaphysical, speculative and legal works fully entitle him to all the credit that he claims for himself as a man of most industrious habit. Shakespeare earned the same reputation. Webster—a writer of that day, connected with the theatrical company—speaks of his "happy, copious industry." Would it not then be beyond the reach of possibility that Bacon would cite his published works as the evidence of a life-time of diligent labour, and express a hope and a doubt as to being able to finish his work before his death, speaking regretfully of the time he had been obliged to lose on account of indifferent health, his determination to publish everything he had time to perfect, and begrudging the time, talent and fortunes expended by others upon works of imagination, "which only led to confusion," if he, in addition to his published works, was the author of works of imagination fully equal in size to everything he claimed, his legal works perhaps excepted? It must be borne in mind that, although Bacon was sixty-six years of age when he died, the writing of the plays did not extend over all that time; in fact, the plays (thirty-seven in number) and the sonnets and poems were written within about eighteen years. How much time does any one think the writer of those plays had for other work? and how does any one suppose such an immense accomplishment could be performed secretly?

If Bacon had possessed any dramatic ability, certainly Ben Jonson would have known it, and he is the one whom it would be reasonable to suppose Bacon would have chosen as the most suitable to put the plays on the stage. Between them there was certainly some bond of literary sympathy. Jonson admired Bacon as a debater, and also assisted him with his Latin translations. Bacon evidently had no sympathy with Jonson's dramatic taste and profession; but if it had been otherwise, and Bacon had been secretly interested in such "toys" and feared to have it known, the most natural thing would have been for him to take Jonson into his confidence and profit by his connection with the stage and the court masques.

It is not easy to imagine grounds upon which it can be urged, that at any time it would have impaired Bacon's political aspirations, to be known as the author of the sonnets, or historical plays. It is not supposable that Queen Elizabeth or any of the persons about the court, would have found it derogatory to his character, or dignity, to have written the sonnets dedicated to Southampton, Essex's nearest friend. That was the kind of accomplishment that commanded high respect at that time. Raleigh, Sydney and Spenser are examples. The profession of actor was held in low esteem, but poetry was highly prized. Authorship, learning and literature were the general ambition. In order to sustain the Baconite theory, it is necessary to falsify the spirit of the time and to invest the people with a sentiment that did not exist. Probably nothing could have advanced Bacon in the favour of Queen Elizabeth so much as just such writings as the sonnets. She cared nothing for Bacon, although he had the prestige of her favourable regard for his father, and she had known him from boyhood. Essex petitioned her in vain for years, for an appointment for him, "while the latter hung about the court." Finally it annoyed her so much that she told him on one occasion to "go to bed if he could talk of nothing but Bacon." Then he, in concert with Bacon, adopted the plan of disparaging other applicants. When Bacon was arrested for a debt of £300 due to a goldsmith, he tried to get her to pay it, and wanted to retaliate upon his creditor by urging that, as he was on business for her majesty at the Tower at the time, it was a misdemeanor in the man to arrest him. The queen on one occasion gave Essex £5,000 worth of cochineal, and also cancelled bonds of immense amount for him, and it is said, at another time paid £20,000 of his debts, but she did not heed Bacon's appeal for only £300, and allowed him to lie in a spunging-house for a paltry debt; at one time she forbade him to enter the court. In the succeeding reign of James I., when most of the plays were on the stage, Bacon rose to political eminence, but he never overcame Queen Elizabeth's dislike. As so much is made of his attainments, there may be an impression that he held some honourable place under the queen, which he feared to jeopard. That is not true. The likelihood is, that the methodical, metaphysical bent of his mind, his servility, egotism, and his prosy homilies were the real obstacles. His Essay on Love was a thousand times more fatal to his connection with the court of Elizabeth, than any dramatic genius could be. The "child of folly" was always a welcome guest there, and there were no courtiers who used their eyes only for the "study of the heavens."

It is much more likely that the utter absence in him of the sentiment of the plays, poems and sonnets of Shakespeare was the cause of Queen Elizabeth's dislike, than that such productions would have hurt his standing at court. She was not the woman to admire his Essay on Love any more than did the widow Hatton, or to be drawn to a man who could treat Cupid as a "corpuscle" and as "primitive matter," and explain why he did not wear clothes. She employed him to write a justification of the execution of Essex and paid him £1,200 for his services in that heartless proceeding; but as she grieved so terribly that the ring, that would have saved the life of Essex, had miscarried, it cannot be otherwise, than that she thoroughly despised Bacon for his part in the tragedy.

The claim that is made upon the plays must include the sonnets. If it is admitted that Shakespeare wrote the sonnets, then the charge of illiteracy is refuted and his ability conceded, and the whole structure of the Baconites' myth is destroyed. The ingenious invention of a cause for concealment as a playwright, does not apply to the sonnets, and it does not explain why, if Bacon had any poetic passion, he should not have contributed to the poetry of the day. A newspaper critic disbelieves in Shakespeare, partly because he did not publish his plays; because he did "not write prefaces for them," and because he did "not appoint Heminge and Condell his literary executors." That cannot be said of the sonnets, Venus and Adonis, and Lucrece. These he published over his own name, prefaced, and dedicated to his friends.

"In the year 1593, Shakespeare printed his Venus and Adonis. His printer was Richard Field, son of Henry Field, tanner, of Stratford-on-Avon, who died in 1592. The inventory of his goods, attached to his will, had been taken by Shakespeare's father in that same year. Shakespeare's choice of a publisher was no doubt influenced by private connection" (Fleay).

If this writer makes it an argument against Shakespeare that he did *not* do certain things in regard to the plays, by the same reasoning he must admit it as a proof in favour of his authorship that he *did* do those things in other writings ; hence as it is proved that he wrote the sonnets, there is no argument left against his authorship of the plays, and no just or reasonable doubters.

Another striking contrast between these men is Shakespeare's thrift and Bacon's improvidence and debt. It is too lengthy a story to give details of Bacon's life-long pecuniary troubles. He was always borrowing. His mother and his brother Anthony were continually devising ways to pay his debts and keep his expenses within bounds. Those who care to get a glimpse into his disgraceful money transactions will find some account of them in Abbott's "Bacon and Essex." Macaulay says, "After his sentence was remitted the government allowed him a pension of £1,200 a year. Unhappily he was fond of display and unused to pay minute attention to domestic affairs. He was not easily persuaded to give up any of the magnificence to which he had been accustomed in the time of his power and prosperity. No pressure of distress could induce him to part with the woods of Gorhambury. 'I will not,' he said 'be stripped of my feathers.' He travelled with so splendid an equipage and so large a retinue that Prince Charles, who once fell in with him on the road, exclaimed with surprise, 'Well! do what we can, this man scorns to go out in snuff.'"

After reading this stricture of so fair a commentator, no one can believe him the author of—

"*Pol.*—Neither a borrower, nor a lender be :
For loan oft loses both itself and friend ;
And borrowing dulls the edge of husbandry."

Bacon did not believe in that interpretation of good husbandry; his life was full of schemes to obtain money as best he could, and to escape the demands of creditors. To further illustrate the comparison between his propensities and the quotation from Shakespeare, just given! In 1624, after his pardon, Bacon had the effrontery to write to Buckingham, " Neither has there been anything done for me that I might die out of ignominy, or live out of want. . . . I firmly hope your grace will deal with his majesty, that as I have tasted of his mercy, I may taste of his bounty." A month later he petitioned the king to the same effect, imploring, for his urgent necessities, three years' advance of his pension, which the king generously granted. King James died in 1625, so that it must have been within a year after this piteous appeal for a practical loan, that Prince Charles met him flourishing in such state; possibly on the proceeds of the advance. Bacon died in 1626, one year later, £22,000 in debt.

After citing his behaviour toward Essex, it is not necessary to give anything further to show his entire lack of every sense of obligation; but that was a monster iniquity; to show the complete absence in his composition, of even a small spirit of thankfulness, his considering that in the remission of his fearful sentence and heavy fine, nothing had been done for him, is well supplemented by the fact, that after the king had granted the advance of money, Bacon wrote Buckingham that there were warrants on the treasury prior to his, and, "as the exchequer is thought to be somewhat barren," urged the duke to use his personal influence with the chancellor to obtain immediate payment, as the other warrants were for gifts, *his was a bargain*.

This is the man who is represented by some of his most active admirers, as so sensitive of his reputation, that he concealed his identity as author of the works of Shakespeare.

It is doubtful if a parallel to Bacon can be found in such utter deficiency of those noble traits, in laudation of which, Shakespeare's utterances have become proverbs.

CHAPTER VII.

Court favourites as patrons of the stage—Shakespeare's industry and property in the plays—Bacon's manuscript—Bacon's experiment with the fowl—Bacon's whereabouts when the plays were collected—Adverse criticism upon Shakespeare—The classics—Bacon and the poem of Lucrece—The Promus.

WHILE Shakespeare's detractors stand amazed that one of such obscure origin and supposed meagre opportunities, should be credited with the masterpieces of English literature, they do not seem conscious of anything singular or unlikely in their theory of Bacon's choice of him as their presumed author. If Shakespeare was an "illiterate man, a ne'er-do-well, and a lounger in tap-rooms," it is not complimentary to their idol's common sense that he should have selected a person of these negative qualifications to produce, for one so jealous of fame and reputation, works of a character that would have excited unbounded surprise and incredulity, especially among his associates and the several rival, and even hostile, playwriters of the day. Neither the quality of the compositions, nor the extent of the work could have been imposed upon Shakespeare's intimates and rivals, by an illiterate ignoramus, or an idle lounger.

The palpable inconsistency of such conditions of origin and development of the plays, does not seem to have presented itself to the minds of Bacon's champions, who are so blinded by an impetuous determination to fix the laurels upon the brow of their oracle, that they race over all impediments without concern as to their number or nature, or as to the inextricable tangle into which they may be led. To give any feature of probability to their assumption, the facts that are well known as to both of the men and the plays make it imperative that the connection between them must have begun soon after Shakespeare's arrival in London, while he was yet an unknown and obscure person, restrained to a position in which he must escape entirely the observation, or even the casual notice, of a man like Bacon, intently bent upon courting favour and recognition only in the highest circles, and fastidious as to his intercourse, or contact, with any people so much in disrepute as actors and players then were. Neither had Bacon, at that time, won any distinction to attract the notice of Shakespeare, or displayed any trait that could imbue the poor player with the belief that Bacon was a man of deep poetic nature, fired with dramatic power struggling to burst into action, and that he might bring these great powers under control so as to convert them to benefits for himself. It is attributing too profound a sagacity to this newly arrived countryman to invest him with such wonderful penetration, such shrewdness and far reaching vision; with the boldness to undertake a scheme for controlling to himself—a poor, unknown youth—the mental gifts, genius and future fame of a proud, ambitious patrician, whose ardent aspirations impelled him in a different direction.

In this Bacon's champions array Shakespeare in a mantle of judgment and wisdom, and crown him with powers of mind, far in excess of those denied him in their disputation of his authorship, while they disparage the intelligence of Bacon by portraying him bartering such precious natural gifts to one who, at that time, had no established reputation, as either actor, manager, playwright, or man; who was merely a supernumerary without money or influence, possessed of no patronage to insure success, or means to guarantee profit; such a transaction would have been as remarkable for stupidity in Bacon as for sagacity in Shakespeare.

The reason urged for concealment on the part of Bacon is equally ludicrous with the hypothesis of collusion between two men so dissimilar in every feature of their existence, deficient in every requisite for mutual attraction, and lacking motive, as well as opportunity, for association. It will be found quite as difficult to reconcile with common sense, the assumption that Bacon feared adverse effect upon his success at court. The Earl of Leicester, the favourite of Queen Elizabeth, was the patron of the company of players that visited Stratford in 1587, with whom Shakespeare is supposed to have left Stratford. Lord Strange, afterwards Earl of Derby, next became its patron, and so remained until his death, when the company received the favour of Lord Hunsdon, who held the post of Lord Chamberlain. The Earls of Hertford, Sussex, and Pembroke, as well as other noblemen, each had a company of players under patronage, and each company bore the name of its patron. It would have taken nothing from Bacon's prestige to have been known as aiding by his wit the purpose of these players, as these prominent noblemen were doing with their names and money. Essex—Bacon's benefactor and the queen's later favourite — wrote a masque. George Villiers, Duke of Buckingham—the favourite of James I. and whose servile tool Bacon was—wrote a play : The Rehearsal. Bacon could not have feared damage to his reputation, or to his prospects, by exposure in the same field of literature with the two men whose favour he begged, and whose gifts he lived upon nearly all his life.

Nothing could be more absurd than to suppose that the court taste was for science or moral essays. Shakespeare's plays were incomparably better received at court than Bacon's writings. What Bacon needed to commend him at court was the exhibition of such gifts, and not the concealment of them.

The supposition that Bacon wrote the plays and concealed his authorship through his desire for political advancement (although it has no force at any time) reaches absurdity when applied to the period after his disgrace. His political career was then at an end, he was sixty years old and could not hope for any further honours. Shakespeare had been dead four years. If fear of marring his prospects had previously prevented him from writing *any* poetry whatever, he had no longer need to suppress his talent. He was released from the Tower and exiled in his house at Gorhambury, and during this time he wrote the versification of the psalms; the papers advocating a new religious crusade and a war for spoils, in the latter of which he described the rich mines of South America as the prospective plunder—which shows that his disgrace and banishment had neither shamed nor humanized him. This was his situation and employment at the time Heminge and Condell were busy collecting the plays and publishing them.

When Bacon wrote his last letter, in which he said his fingers were so stiff he could hardly hold a pen, he mentioned the experiment of stuffing the fowl with snow (which caused his death), and said the experiment succeeded remarkably well. This letter he wrote when he knew he was going to die, and in it he compares himself to the elder Pliny, who lost his life while exploring Vesuvius. That was the time, if he had a weighty secret on his mind, that he would have divulged it. Just then one line from him, that he was the author of the plays, would have registered his claim, and his right to the title would have been proved, or disproved, before Shakespeare's friends had passed away. It would be difficult to find a more marked instance of the "ruling passion strong in death" than Bacon's reference to this experiment when he knew it had been fatal to him; especially as it indicates that he must have made inquiry as to its results in the meantime, as his sudden illness prevented any personal investigation. His interest and curiosity in that kind of investigation was so great that he could only relinquish it with his life, and he made it the subject of a letter when he was struck with death.

The whole of Shakespeare's productions had less interest to Bacon and less value in his estimation than the experiment of snow as an antiseptic, and there is nothing to induce a belief that he considered Shakespeare or his art of sufficient importance to interrupt his "serious observations." The circumstances that caused his death, and his dying testimony as to his absorbing interest in scientific research, are conclusive as to the kind of subjects that occupied his mind, to the exclusion of all others.

If Shakespeare was but little known in his time, it argues that his plays held no very high place in the estimation of the "better sort," whatever their popularity with the mass, and this fact is attested by much general evidence. They had no marked popularity with the great, or promise of it, to attract Bacon's attention, or tempt his cupidity.

The people who played such prominent parts in the politics of that age had no thought that the events in which they figured would become so familiar to posterity from the presence among them of a man whose calling they esteemed so little, whose genius they so inadequately recognised, and whose period of activity was so short. It is true that the plays drew large audiences. Leonard Digges, born 1588, wrote in 1640 that "when the audiences saw Shakespeare's plays, they were ravished and went away in wonder; and although Ben Jonson was admired, yet when his best plays would hardly bring money enough to pay for sea-coal fire, Shakespeare's would fill cock-pit, galleries, boxes, and scarce leave standing room." The plays were well received at court, but they were popular among the people. The indication is, however, that those who wrote and figured in the political history of that time did not regard the theatre as of public interest, and did not expect it to lend any fame to their epoch.

It seems as though the audiences at the theatre appreciated Shakespeare, but they were not the people who have left any record. As evidence that the plays received no favour at that time, of a kind to attract Bacon, I quote, from well-known names, the following criticisms: "Shakespeare is a wit out of date and unintelligible" (Dryden). "A wit out of fashion, a coarse and savage mind" (Shaftesbury). "He had neither tragic nor comic talent. Nothing equals the absurdity of such a spectacle as the witches in Macbeth" (Forbes). "The comic in Shakespeare is too heavy, and does not make one laugh" (Foote). "The comic in Shakespeare is altogether low, and very inferior to Shadwell" (Warburton). "Voltaire qualifies the scene of the grave-diggers as the follies, characterizes the pieces as monstrous farces, declares that Shakespeare ruined the English theatre, calls him a barbarian, and wants to be delivered from that ninny Shakespeare" (Hugo). Hume says of him, "It is in vain that we look for purity or simplicity of diction. He is totally ignorant of all theatrical art and conduct, deficient in taste, elegance, harmony and correctness;" and concludes, "Ever since the English theatre has taken a strong tincture of Shakespeare's spirit and character; and thence it has proceeded that the nation has undergone from all its neighbours the reproach of barbarism, from which its valuable productions in some other parts of learning would otherwise have exempted it." "In 1725 Pope finds a reason why Shakespeare wrote his dramas. 'One must eat'" (Hugo). Blount and Jaggard struck out of Hamlet alone (1623 edition) two hundred lines; also two hundred and twenty-four lines out of King Lear. "In 1707 one called Nahun Tate published a 'King Lear,' warning his readers that he had borrowed the idea from a play he had read by chance, the work of some unknown author. The unknown author was Shakespeare" (Hugo). Tate was born 1652; died 1716. "He produced an alteration of Shakespeare's King Lear, which long held the stage to the exclusion of the original" (Appleton's Encyclopædia). Garrick played Tate's King Lear. George III. declared Shakespeare "poor stuff." Pepys declared the Midsummer Night's Dream the most insipid, ridiculous play that he ever saw in his life; Romeo and Juliet the worst; Twelfth Night silly, having no relation to the name or day; and Macbeth a most excellent play for variety. A book called the Golden Medley, published in 1720, informed its readers that, "if it had not been for Shakespeare's Tempest, he would scarce have been allowed a place among the dramatic poets." "Addison left Shakespeare unnamed in his Account of the Greatest English Poets" (June Temple Bar). Green says he is a plagiarist, a copyist, has invented nothing, is a crow adorned with the plumes of others. He pilfers from a dozen writers, which he names, himself among the number. Nothing is his. He is a blower of verses, a shake-scene, a Johannes factotum. Thomas Rymer says, "What edifying and useful impression can an audience receive from such poetry? To what can this poetry serve, unless it is to mislead our good sense, to throw our thoughts into disorder, to trouble our brain, to pervert our instincts, to crack our imaginations, to corrupt our tastes, and fill our hearts with variety, confusion, clatter and nonsense?" I have copied these adverse criticisms upon Shakespeare in order to show that he had no standing or reputation that would attract Bacon or awaken in him any desire for fame from such a source. The stage promised neither present profit nor future renown.

Macaulay says Bacon was never charged by any accuser, entitled to the smallest credit, with licentious habits. How is it possible to associate such sentiment as the poem of Lucrece and many of the plays contain, with a man whose nature is so cold that his description of love fills the object of his "choice" with dread and alarm! If his love essay is his honest thought, then it is impossible to suppose him the author of any love poem or scene, and especially one of Shakespeare's. He strove for the reputation

of wisdom, gravity; for veneration, and for
fame in history. The condemnation of all that
was embraced in stage acting as corrupt, and
of sensual poetry or anything tending to lascivi-
ousness, was a part of his profession. Such
things as his admirers are seeking to adorn him
with would have been repugnant to his nature,
and have shown him thoughtless of his dignity,
careless of his ambition and forgetful of his
reputation. The attempt to prove that Bacon
was in sympathy with the stage and play acting
is everywhere contradicted by his expressions
of distaste for it.

It will not be admitted by any one that the
writer of the plays could have been devoid of
the spirit that pervades them, or indifferent
about their success. Their music could never
be as sweet, their humour as delightful, their
philosophy as true, or their people as natural, if
they had been the work of a man who had no
conscience in his art or kindred in his characters.
It is impossible that one whose nature was not
overflowing with the spirit of romance, poetry
and adventure, and who was not inspired with
a love of the creations of his fancy and imagination, could have touched the human heart as
Shakespeare has done.

While some people of the present day are so incredulous as to Shakespeare's learning, and so unwilling to admit that he possessed sufficient familiarity with the literature of his day to have produced his works, it is reassuring to contrast their doubts with the attacks made upon him by his rival contemporaries. Greene, for instance, who knew Shakespeare well, and "whose Pandosto afforded Shakespeare the plot for his Winter's Tale," charges him with pilfering from Æschylus, Boccaccio, Bandello, Holinshed, Belleforest, Benoit de St. Maur, Lugamon, Robert of Gloucester, Robert of Wace, Peter of Longtoft, Robert Manning, John de Mandeville, Sackville, Spenser, Sidney, Rowley, Dekker and Chettle.

It is remarkable that poor Greene in his jealousy of Shakespeare should have furnished such an unintentional denial of the charge of Shakespeare's illiteracy. It would be absurd to suppose that he would accuse him of pilfering from these sources if he did not know them to be accessible to him. It is more than doubtful if it required a familiarity with the classics to become familiar with these authors, as they were probably, all to some extent translated into English. While Bacon was travelling back toward antiquity, there were others who were arraying the ancients in English costume. "The three Roman plays, Coriolanus, Julius Cæsar and Antony and Cleopatra, were derived from North's *translation* of Plutarch's Lives (1579); Troilus and Cressida from Ludgate's Troy Book (printed 1513, and Chapman's *translation* of Homer (1596). All's Well that Ends Well, from a *translation* of Painter's Palace of Pleasure, of the ninth novel of the third day of Boccaccio's Decameron. The story of Much Ado about Nothing is found in Spenser's Faerie Queene, founded upon a story in Ariosto's Orlando Furioso (1516)." By these dates we know that Homer, Plutarch and Boccaccio were translated before these plays were written. The seven historical plays, also King Lear and Macbeth, were drawn from the Chronicles of Holinshed. There is nothing to prove that Shakespeare did not read languages with as much ease as Bacon. Such knowledge was more common then than now. The facilities for acquiring it were abundant. Priests, monks and school-masters were proficients. Pope is an apt illustration, although somewhat later.

Encyclopædia Britannica says of him, "The delicate child's book-education was desultory and irregular. His father's religion excluded him from the public schools. Before he was twelve he got a smattering of Latin and Greek from various masters, from a priest at Hampshire, from a school-master at Twyford, from another at Marlebone, from a third at Hyde Park Corner, and finally from another priest at home. He thought himself the better in some respects for not having had a regular education."

The tenor of the Baconites' argument induces either a doubt as to their belief in natural genius, or a conviction that they believe Bacon possessed it all. It would be awarding them too little ordinary intelligence to adopt the latter proposition, in spite of their bigoted admiration. The drift of Bacon's reasoning is in the other direction, and placing them in harmony with him, it is fair to assume that the alternative, a disbelief in genius, is the position they hold. This involves the necessity of admitting that Bacon had no genius, and that if his sphere had been the same as Shakespeare's, he would have achieved no fame as a writer or thinker. If then his knowledge and learning are to be credited with all that these people claim for him, how little of the ground for their claims is left, may be judged by the following analysis of Bacon, made by Professor Draper, in his Intellectual Development of Europe : " The more closely we examine the writings of Lord Bacon, the more unworthy does he seem to have been of the great reputation which has been awarded him. . . . This boasted founder of a new philosophy could not comprehend, and would not accept, the greatest of all scientific doctrines when it was plainly set before his eyes. . . . Bacon never produced any great practical result himself, no great physicist has ever made any use of his method. . . . Of all the important physical discoveries, there is not one which shows that its author made it by the Baconian instrument. He rejected the Copernican system and spoke insolently of its great author ; he undertook to criticise adversely Gilbert's treatise ' De Magnete ;' he was occupied in the condemnation of any investigation of final causes, while Harvey was deducting the circulation of the blood. . . . Newton never seems to have been aware that he was under any obligation to

Bacon. . . . Few scientific pretenders have made more mistakes than Lord Bacon, . . . He was doubtful whether instruments were any advantage, while Galileo was investigating the heavens with the telescope. Ignorant himself in every branch of mathematics, he presumed that they were useless in science but a few years before Newton achieved, by their aid, his immortal discoveries. It is time that the sacred name of philosophy should be severed from its long connection with that of one who was a pretender of science, a time serving politician, an insiduous lawyer, a corrupt judge, a treacherous friend and a bad man."

It would be refreshing to know from the Baconian doubters of genius, how they account for such children as Pope, Macaulay, Jeremy Bentham (who studied Latin at the age of three, French conversation at five, and was matriculated at college at thirteen), or such a prodigy as Crichton, whose skill, intellectually and physically, verged on enchantment, and for hosts of others who have exhibited precocious and marvellous development of individual traits and faculties. They cannot expect, by such argument, to convince a well-read generation that Shakespeare could not have written the plays owing to the difficulty of acquiring a reading knowledge of languages that, in his day, every school-master understood, and which were the fashion of the time. Even poor Greene seems to have possessed the linguistic knowledge, the supposed lack of which has furnished an argument for the writing of volumes to prove Shakespeare could not have written the plays. The writings of Shakespeare's detractors abound in references to Bacon's biographers, and they endeavour by insinuation to make it appear that these partially favour their theory. This is absolutely unfounded. There is no shadow for such an impression. They are full believers in Shakespeare, and Devey says he created a new language.

Some of the most empty volumes that have appeared on this branch of the subject, are by a judge, who bases his argument upon the weak premise of Shakespeare's inability to acquire a reading knowledge of Latin ; an acquisition in which he takes good care to leave readers in no doubt as to his own proficiency. It is to be hoped that this luminous individual will prove the potency of Latin, by giving us something equal to Shakespeare ; possibly he has already tossed it off, and only delays it to incorporate a cipher. I pray him to relieve suspense, and let us have at once this proof of the dead tongue's power to inspire the sublimest thought.

Upon this phase of the question, however, the Baconites are at variance with Bacon himself, which is something of an argument that they do not read his works. In his Advancement of Learning he says, "And to say the truth, the reason why the excellent writings and moral discourses of the ancients have so little effect upon our lives and manners, seems to be that they are not read by men of ripe age and judgment, but wholly left to inexperienced youths and children." This is quite conclusive that if the classics were not then translated into English, Bacon had no knowledge of the inability of youths and children to acquire the language in which they were written. These modern linguists are possibly so sharpened in perception by their studies, that they can pierce the veil of time, much more effectually than Bacon could comprehend his own surroundings.

I note one writer who will not believe that

Shakespeare was not a member of the club that met at the "Mermaid" Tavern, which was founded by Sir Walter Raleigh and attended by some celebrated men, although Shakespeare's name does not appear among them. It is quite in keeping with the argument of people who insist that the appearance of Shakespeare's name in connection with the plays is no proof of his authorship; to aver with equal boldness that the non-appearance of his name on a club roll is good proof of his membership. There is no need to suppose him spending his time in dissipation and club revels, and there is no data whatever for such an accusation. The little that is told of him outside of his domain of labour, may be explained by his extraordinary industry and untiring devotion to his purpose. The voluminous work he did in so short a time is an all-sufficient answer to the charge of his being an idler; the accumulation of a competence in so precarious a business, a refutation of his being a dissipated spendthrift, as well as testimony to the value of his services to the company, to which he adhered with a tenacity that well bespeaks the man who wrote—

"The friends thou hast, and their adoption tried,
Grapple them to thy soul with hoops of steel."

He produced at the rate of two plays a year for seventeen years, besides his other pieces, and travelled with his company; during which time the company had to contend with opposition and prejudice, and were often hindered by the plague. The amount of work he did, not only attests the most unremitting study and application, but it verifies what Heminge and Condell said of him, "His mind and hand went together; what he thought he uttered with that easiness, that we have scarce received from him a blot in his papers." Such work could not have been done laboriously. If he had been the roystering fellow that many persist in calling him, he would be far better known to-day as to his personality; but in those times people did not seek to discover "patient merit," and a man whose whole thought and interest were in his art, might attract but little attention and have few friends outside of his profession. The slurs that are flung at his character are relics of the prejudice against the stage which has not yet passed away; the doubt that pioneers the incredulity has its origin in an unwillingness that a man of such a calling shall "bear the palm alone." As the world grows to an appreciation of the moral worth of Shakespeare's philosophy, there will be a recast of the judgment of what the stage has done for civilization.

If Shakespeare neglected to publish his plays, it may be accounted for by many suppositions. The plays were not entirely new. Many of them existed in some form before, and were rewritten by him. Some are thought to be only partly his. In the early part of his time it is said that Marlowe, and other playwrights, wrote in conjunction with him. The plots of some were old, and perhaps much of the framework was retained; in some cases more than one story was woven into a play. A man of Shakespeare's "uprightness of dealing which argueth his honesty" might naturally be unwilling to collect the plays and assert his ownership of what must have seemed to be the common property of a company that had worked together to put them upon the stage. This, of course, is conjecture, but is worth whatever of probability it may suggest; one can easily imagine a disturbing of the comradeship that might ensue from such a course, and this, the affection and good fellowship that

P

existed between Shakespeare and his fellows, would forbid.

It is a question also whether, if Shakespeare furnished the plays and was paid for them, *he* and his colleagues did not consider them the property of the theatre. There may have been many reasons why they were not published, chief of all the expense and doubtful return; but as no one ever questioned Shakespeare's authorship, and no one else ever claimed it, the fact of the neglect that attended the plays cannot be cited as casting any doubt upon the reputed author. Certainly they were all produced by his company while he was its playwright, and every actor, as well as every other writer and publisher, believed him the author.

How different this carelessness about the manuscripts, from Bacon's practice! He treasured every scratch of his pen. The accounts of his petty expenses, the names of one hundred and fifty servants, a minute memorandum of the symptoms of a fit of indigestion, have been published. Even the notes, exclamations and apparently meaningless words that he jotted down for future use, from the books that he had read, or plays he had seen, and his random scribblings, were preserved by him and are now in the British Museum. He would not have allowed his writings to be handled as these plays were; the printers rejecting, accepting and mutilating them according to their own judgment. Bacon's waste-basket was, in his own conceit, filled with pearls; every scrap of memorandum had a gilt edge, as it were. One cannot suppose him suffering the children of his imagination to lie about in dirt and dust, behind the scenes of a theatre, at the haphazard care of actors, and caught up finally, by chance and in fragments, to be published under the dictum of the printers, and that, too, in an insular tongue that he did not believe would survive the next generation.

His love of order alone would have forbidden such carelessness with his manuscripts. It is said that everything that he wrote was kept with great care by his secretary in a cabinet in his library. That order was his habit, frequent instances in his writings attest. In his Essay on Masques he says, "They are nothing unless the room be well kept and clean." In the tirsan's feast the room is "well kept and without disorder." In the entry of the sage they had no horsemen in the procession, fearing it would cause disorder, and the "street was wonderfully well kept;" the people did not jostle each other at the windows, but "stood as if they had been placed."

The disregard of the value of the manuscripts, or delay about printing them, which allowed them to lie at the risk of loss, injury and destruction, from whatever cause it arose, cannot be reconciled with Bacon's watchful care and preservation of all his productions. He preserved even the beginnings and introductions to articles that were never finished, and also copies of his letters, and directed in his will that all should be published.

These commands have been scrupulously observed, and all these relics are watchfully kept in the British Museum, where people of a certain class regard them with about the same feelings as those of another sort, in another department of the same institution, look upon a mummy case, or an Assyrian tablet: and with about the same degree of comprehension.

In the articles which have been written to show parallels between Shakespeare and Bacon, the former, almost without exception, is in verse and the latter *always* in prose. There is never any comparison of style, but it is the subject and the similarity of certain words to which attention is called, and even then it is often difficult to discover the similitude. It is very far-sought comparison to endeavour to prove that Bacon wrote Shakespeare's plays by evidence that the writer of the plays had a knowledge of the authors that Bacon has *copied* in his memorandums; especially as these writings were mostly translated, and, when not, translators were easily found. These resemblances are mostly cited in what has been styled Bacon's Promus, which is a collection of notes. (over 1600) that he jotted down for future use, from what he read and heard. They are not sketches; and among them all there is not a hint of the story or plot of one of Shakespeare's plays. Every one must appreciate the need of notes to an author. Fancy is a mistress full of moods, to whose visits, whenever they may chance to come, her votaries are always attentive, and incidents are vivid when they are fresh. I have read some of Hawthorne's notes that were stories in embryo; but Bacon's notes were not fancies or incidents: they were words, exclamations and sentences. They had about the same relation to the article in which they might afterwards appear as Mr. Vincent Crummles' "real pump and washing-tubs" had to the prospective play that Nickleby might write, and many of them were about as wooden: a school-boy sort of trick of saving up a lot of words to eke out compositions and produce effects. They were his veritable "apparatus of rhetoric;" the "doors, windows, staircases and back rooms to be skilfully contrived." They were not his own thoughts, but material that he picked up to be worked into anything that he might have in hand, and they account for what I have said in a previous chapter of his extraordinary habit of quotation. They are the things Bacon calls "unmade up." When the meaningless and ordinary character of much of this Promus collection is considered, it will show my description to be reasonable, indeed, these notes are of so promiscuous a character that even Spedding, Bacon's greatest admirer, says "it is sometimes difficult to understand why these particular lines should have been taken and so many others, apparently of equal merit, passed by;" but he accounts for it by the most flattering conjecture, and seems to have no doubt but when the expressions come to be "made up" Bacon will fully justify himself.

These sheets, called Promus, from that word written on one of them, are fifty in number and are almost without matter of interest. They contain nothing that is not accessible from other and better sources, and, I may even say, that is not familiar to every one of fair education ; a great portion of the entries is of the most common-place, every-day words and expressions ; the remainder, proverbs, sayings in general use, and quotations from a few well-known sources. Only to those who consider work on a tread-mill, or breaking stones on the road, delightful pastime, would I recommend a perusal.

Whatever Bacon touched has such a charm for some minds, however, that one of his most ardent admirers has expanded these few dry leaves into a bulky volume of over six hundred pages, in an effort to convert them into duplicate parts of Shakespeare's plays. This work endeavours to fit parts of the plays to nearly every word, phrase, or turn of thought found in these leaves of Bacon's memoranda, yet there is not a pen mark in them that contains any allusion to a character, a plot, an incident, a stage direction, a stage costume or property, or to a living actor, or any other thing belonging to any one of Shakespeare's plays.

It greatly curtails a controversy when one side is anxious to aid the other in bringing forward its evidence and securing for it the undiverted attention of the tribunal ; this, every friend of the plays must desire for this exhibit of Bacon in "his worshop" of "unmade," teeming with its convicting proof that the man who made such a collection could not command either ease, freedom, spontaneity, or originality in his work : that poetic fervour and tender sentiment could not draw an inspiration, or a breath of life; the player's passion receive a ray of cheering warmth, nor his heart a single prompting, from such a jumbled medley of odds and ends. If I were trying to prove Bacon the writer of the plays I should wish the Promus not his, or that it might not come to light. Without intended discourtesy, or disregard of the respect due to one who has performed so much labour in proof of her faith, rather than of her case, this book recalls the social amusement, "What is my thought like?" in which one person whispers an object, and another a subject, to each of the company, and then it is the part of each one in turn to describe some resemblance between the two. This is the game that this lady plays in her book. Bacon furnishes her with an object, and in Shakespeare she finds a thought, then fits them together according to the measure of her own cleverness rather than by any inherent similarity; for instance, "polished perturbation," "golden care," and "restless ecstacy" as descriptive of ill lodging. Those who have played at this game with clever people will remember what unexpected and extraordinary resemblances are often discovered, and also what ingenious absurdities can be concocted. It was not necessary, however, to take the Promus for this purpose. There are many books that would have been infinitely more suitable. When Shakespeare's plays are before one, it is possible to find some suspicion of a resemblance to almost any word or expression in the English language. No one with the fancy to write Mother Goose would need to have his imagination prodded or his "understanding twitched" by such a medley of ordinary and unsuggestive notes. They indicate that Bacon's writing was of a laborious, methodical and mechanical character; and this discovery in the British Museum of Bacon's "preparatory store for the furniture of speech" (Spedding) is calculated to weaken the belief in his originality, rather than to prove him a poet, "with seething brain" and "imagination all compact."

The work is too voluminous to undertake in this small book a detailed illustration or criticism of the examples cited in it to prove similarity, nor is this at all necessary, a few will suffice to show the weakness of the whole. Note 1404 in the Promus is "O the." This most familiar and common form of exclamation, in all time, is then cited as used by Shakespeare in the following instances : "O the heavens !" (Tempest, I. 2, twice). "O the devil !" (Richard III, iv. 3). "O the time !" (Hamlet, v. 1, song). "O the gods !" (Cymbeline, i. 5 ; Coriolanus, iv. 1). "O the good gods !" (Antony and Cleopatra, v. 11). "O the vengeance !" (Hamlet, ii. 2). "O all the devils !" (Cymbeline, i. 5). "O the Lord !" (2d Henry IV., ii. 4.) "O the blest gods !" (King Lear, ii. 4).

Note 1221 in the Promus is "Amen." The authoress then gives a passage from Macbeth in which Amen occurs four times, and a note follows to the effect that the word occurs sixty-three times in the plays.

By such argument as this she could as easily prove that Bacon was the translator of the King James edition of the Bible, the author of the Church Service and of hundreds of hymns. It is wondrous that she could allow to escape, such an opportunity for magnifying Bacon's powers. The probabilities favour his hand in that work, much more than his authorship of Shakespeare. The task was more in the direction of his attainments and powers; merely translations, not composition. Only forty-seven great scholars were occupied on that work about three years, in tolerable seclusion; Shakespeare occupied twenty years, travelled much as a player, and did his work publicly, in connection with ever changing coadjutors. Why not assume the great scholars to have been merely figures and Bacon the quiet performer of their task?

These are a few of the notes that this industrious lady has set forth in an octavo volume of six hundred and twenty-eight pages to show that Bacon wrote the plays. To all of them she has adjusted some Shakespeare passage: (1294) watery impressions; (1312) neutrality; (1230) hot cockles; (1231) good night; (1232) well to forget; (1224) I cannot get out of my good lodging; (1215) uprouse, you are upp; (1213) court howers; (1189) good morrow—ninety-six times in the plays; (1190) good swoear—for its similitude, "good even" occurs eleven times in the plays; (1191) good travaile; (1192) good matens; (1193) good betimes; (1180) betts, lookers on, judgment; (1181) groome, porter; (1183) oddes, stake, sett; (1168) art of forgetting; (1158) abomination; (1153) it is Goddes doing; (1132) for learning sake; (965) no smoke without fire; (964) might overcomes right; (957) we be but where we were; (952) pride will have a fall; (878) an owles egg; (864) armed intreaty; (818) cream of nectar; (718 a) to way ancre.

One of the most emphasized instances of a likeness in the writings is Note 1207, Golden Sleepe. One similarity is:

"Where unbruised youth with unstuffed brain
Doth couch his limbs, there golden sleep doth reign."
—*Romeo and Juliet.*

The question of probability is whether Bacon, seeing Romeo and Juliet, should miss the finer parts of a play in which the "lover thinks so absurdly well of the party loved," and, his ear being caught by the sound of "golden sleepe," he should jot it down for future rhetorical effect, to be "made up" into "frontispieces" of "Traditive Prudence;" or whether, having met with it elsewhere, he should use it as a reminder, in composing verses in which it had no relation to the sense, and was the less striking part, as "golden" could be better spared from these lines than any other word in them.

Shakespeare uses the word "golden" in another instance, not quoted in the Promus.

"Golden lads and girls all must,
As chimney sweepers, come to dust."—*Cymbeline.*

There is rollicking fun in this that may be well contrasted with the mechanical beat of Bacon's strains.

Note 1223 of the Promus is:

"You could not sleepe for y^r yll lodging."

For similarity to this is quoted:

"Why doth the crown lie there upon his pillow,
Being so troublesome a bedfellow?

O polish'd perturbation ! golden care !
That keep'st the ports of slumber open wide
To many a watchful night," etc.
    —*Second Part Henry IV.*, iv. 4.

"(We sleep) in the affliction of these terrible dreams
That shake us nightly. Better be with the dead
Than on the torture of the mind to lie
In restless ecstasy."—*Macbeth.*

All the comment necessary is in the lines.

One of the most conspicuous instances of distance between word and thought is Note 1432 of the Promus, "The Avenues," which it is intimated appears in substance in the following passages of Shakespeare :

"Open thy gate of mercy, gracious lord."
"The gates of mercy shall be all shut up."
"I will lock up all the gates of love."
"Pathways to his will."
"The natural gates and alleys of the body."
"The road of casualty."
"Untread the roadway of rebellion."
"The road into his kindness."
"The way to dusty death."
"(His) grace chalks successors their way."
"The way of loyalty and truth."
"The ways of honour."
"Which lead directly to the door of truth."
  "Having found the back door open
Of the unguarded hearts."

It is stated that the word "Avenues" does not appear in Shakespeare, which shows the liberal scope allowed in grasping the pearls that do appear. A word not used is just as useful for the purpose as one used scores of times.

The true character and little value of these sheets of Bacon's jottings must strike any one familiar with dates and authors, and not blinded by a purpose stronger than reason. As words and phrases become common property so soon, it would require more direct proof than even the fact that Bacon was the originator of what is here found, to establish his title to any work whatever, but when we come to find that the earliest date on these sheets is 1593, and the earliest on them that can be taken to apply distinctly to them is December, 1594,—after Shakespeare had been six to eight years hard at work; when his plays had become popular with the people and had been frequently given before the court;—the utter worthlessness of the Promus, as evidence against him, is fully established, even if no other argument could be brought against it. That it contains merely notes of what Bacon heard, or read, that struck a chord in his projects, is easily discernible.

Take the English Proverbs copied so copiously that two hundred are from one work, that of Heywood, published in 1562—when Bacon was one year old. Of these this lady says, in citing them as proof of Bacon's hand, one hundred and fifty-two appear in the plays; but she does not see that this is a much stronger argument that Heywood wrote the plays than that Bacon did, especially as she says there are forty proverbs in the plays that are not in the Promus. If illustration of these proverbs in the plays must be taken as a clue to authorship, then it must lead to their most immediate, or original possessor, not to the man who merely copied from him.

The profuse copying from Erasmus is quite a trustworthy agent in giving a basis for the date of some of these sheets. Erasmus was one of the most learned and fluent of Latin scholars. He was a genial, easy man, fond of companions and popular, a friend of the reformation and a worker in the cause, but not disposed to risk martyrdom. His works had been interdicted in some countries for their strictures upon the Romish church, but in 1603 a new and most complete edition appeared.

Bacon, by the character of his own pursuits and aspirations, would be naturally attracted to this work, and judging by the general character of the extracts he made, devoted much attention to reading it, this would fix the date of the sheets upon which these quotations appear at not earlier than 1603, possibly somewhat later.

The works of Erasmus would furnish abundant material of the "unmade" sort, and some of Bacon's works give evidence of his ideas and form of expression twisted and turned to embellish points quite unintended by the original; a significant instance is Promus, Note 862, *Quadratus homo*—A square man. That is the literal translation of the expression; and Erasmus defined it to mean, a man well perfected, of even temper and mind, whom adversity and prosperity alike made no impression upon.

Bacon, with his usual false reasoning and tendency to pervert true philosophy, interpreted it to mean "a gull," a man squared for the designs of more cunning men, and he uses it in this form of illustration in one of his works.

The square man of Shakespeare was Horatio, to whom Hamlet says—

> " Since my dear soul was mistress of her choice,
> And could of men distinguish, her election
> Hath seal'd thee for herself; for thou hast been
> As one, in suffering all, that suffers nothing :
> A man, that fortune's buffets and rewards
> Has ta'en with equal thanks : and bless'd are those
> Whose blood and judgment are so well commingled,
> That they are not a pipe for Fortune's finger
> To sound what stop she please. Give me that man
> That is not passion's slave, and I will wear him
> In my heart's core, ay, in my heart of heart,
> As I do thee.—"

The man who tortured the well established, pure meaning of a square man into an emblem of gullibility, was incapable of uttering those lines; and the man who did write them, never hunted to the death a noble self-sacrificing friend like Essex.

These Promus Notes are scarcely worthy of discussion, but they offer great temptation from the boldness with which they have been presented. They afford proof, however, that the vocabulary of Bacon was that of every man who wrote, or uttered, a word or expression that he deemed worthy of appropriation to his own purpose. That they teem with this evidence is the strongest impression they create, but they afford also, from the elaborate illustrations of the lady who edited them, a good opportunity for comparing the style and diction, as well as dramatic sense and comprehension, of the two men. I give a few instances :

Promus, Note 62. *Vincula qui rupit, dedoluitque semel.*

Bacon's deduction—

"Nature is often hidden, sometimes overcome, seldom extinguished. . . . Where nature is mighty and therefore the victory hard, the degrees had need be, first to stay and arrest nature in time, . . . but if a man have the fortitude and resolution to enfranchise himself at once, that is the best."

The Illustrations from Shakespeare—

"If thou hast nature in thee bear it not."—*Hamlet*, i. 5.

"Oh heart, lose not thy nature."—*Hamlet*, iii. 2.

"Refrain to-night
And that shall lend a kind of easiness
To the next abstinence ; the next more easy ;
For use almost can change the stamp of nature
And master the devil, or throw him out
With wondrous potency."—*Hamlet* iii. 4.

Promus, Note 67. *Divitiae impedimenta virtutis.* (The baggage of virtue.)

Bacon's exemplification—

"I cannot call riches better than the baggage of virtue (the Roman is better, 'impedimenta'), for as the baggage is to an army, so riches is to virtue."

Illustration from Shakespeare—
  "If thou art rich, thou'rt poor,
  For like an ass whose back with ingots bows,
  Thou bear'st thy heavy riches but a journey."

Promus, Note 86. Full musicke of easy ayres, without strange concordes and discordes.
Bacon's application—
  "I ever liked the Galenists that deal with good compositions; and not the Parcelsians, that deal with fine separations; and in music I ever loved easy airs, that go full at all the parts together, and not these strange points of accord and discord."

Illustration from Shakespeare—
  "Music do I hear?
  Ha, ha! keep time; how sour sweet music is
  When time is broke, and no proportion kept,
  So is it in the music of men's lives.
  And here have I the daintiness of ear
  To check time broke in a disordered string,
  But for the concord of my state and time,
  Had not an ear to hear my true time broke."

Promus, Note 378. *Bene omnia fecit.* (He hath done all things well.—*Mark*, vii. 37.)
Bacon's application—
  "A true confession and applause. God, when he created all things, saw that every thing in particular, and all things in general, were exceeding good."

Illustrations from Shakespeare—
  "To see how God, in all his creatures works!"

  "Tongues in trees, books in the running brooks,
  Sermons in stones, and good in everything."

The rapture with which Bacon first greets the announcement of this great truth, and then his speedy dismissal of "everything in general," with approval, may be called dramatic, but scarcely poetic.

Poetry is a beautiful form, a creation of perfected unity, and we will not accept the theory, put forth in this book on the Promus, that it can be anatomized and analyzed into its mere elements of speech without destruction or separating the spirit from the body. If we are to attribute the birth of a sublime thought to the inspiration of some word used in its expression, then any man who in Milton's time wrote down the word Satan, may stand in line of being crowned with the authorship of Paradise Lost. That was Bacon's method, he seized upon words and the thoughts of others, and built of them his patched-up structures ; to Shakespeare the whole structure was first a vision, and giving it shape and substance, he built in the mass of elements that, to the other man, were the carved out ornaments of an otherwise homely piece of work.

If Bacon had possessed the great natural gift that belonged to the writer of the plays, it would have been impossible for him to have suppressed in youth every inclination to pen a line of verse, or give vent to a poetic burst; such latent power, like a pent up fountain, would have burst forth at unlooked for places; and if, as is claimed for him, he had a passion for music, it would have flowed in song in spite of his disgust for love. It is not easy though to reconcile a real passion for music with a disgust for its companion sentiment, love. Instead of poetry Bacon's youth brought forth statistics, which is a remarkable likeness in his turn of mind and that of the authoress of Promus, whose book is merely a compilation to show how many times one writer may have used the words and forms of another. This is an endless theme, and may be carried to the extent of as many volumes as there are works to be compared.

The significant feature of these notes; that they contain no marks associating them with, or referring to any of the stories, details, or business of the plays, is brought into striking prominence by the unmistakable evidence of careful, systematic preparation of numbers of them for use in the works Bacon is known to have devoted himself to, as well as by the prevalence of notes and manipulations of words and expressions that he conveyed to the writings upon which he hoped to found a great reputation. From the connection of subject, or the thread denoted by the succession of many of these extracts, it is evident that they are not solely jottings of what he casually heard or read, but are to a considerable extent, excerpts from books that he searched for the purpose of supplying to the subject he had in process, ideas and suggestions which his own mind, from its natural lack of originality and creative power, failed to furnish.

To this, in addition to his regard for everything his pen touched, may be traced the preservation of these sheets among his valued papers, but it is an unfavourable comment upon his sanity to parade these hoarded scribblings, and at the same time assert that he scattered to the winds the great harvest of which they are but the seeds. He was not the man who, after building a lovely palace, would obliterate every vestige and treasure up merely the debris.

The signature to Shakespeare's will, written

shortly before his death—under what circumstances no one will presume to know—has been dilated upon as an evidence that he could not have written the plays. If the last letter that Bacon wrote, when he said his fingers were so stiff he could scarcely hold the pen, be compared with this signature, it will be found that an equally plausible argument can be adduced against him, and this can be urged with augmented force against the chirography of the Promus MSS. The players undoubtedly learned their *rôles* from Shakespeare's manuscripts, but I defy them to have accomplished that much from such penmanship as fills these sheets.

A lithographed copy of one of them has been attached by the authoress to the fly leaves of her book, but for what purpose no one can well divine as she does not allude to it, that I can discover, anywhere in her comments. It may be intended as a charm, or to impress the on-looker with what frantic dashes Bacon's fancy marked the sheet, before he brought it to subjugation under the strokes of his invincible pen. Its object may be to illustrate how the "apparatus of rhetoric" tore up the earth and scattered the fragments, when that ponderous engine began to move on one of its journeys of demolition against "all the systems of philosophy hitherto received or imagined." The unsophisticated may stand in wonder as to whether it is the letter about the chicken experiment, or the key that solves the magic tongue mentioned in the New Atlantis, which "Hebrews, Persians and Indians could read as if written in their own language."

It would be pleasant to accord to this book the fair intention of arriving at the truth which is claimed for it, but it is inconsistent with that claim, to contemn a natural suggestion that Bacon may have copied from Shakespeare ; to distort such evidence leading in that direction as incidentally crops out, and to suppress other that is within reach or obtainable. A prominent instance of such effort is the citation of Bacon's use, in a letter to King James, of the expression "love must creep where it cannot go," which is an adoption of Shakespeare's phrase in the Two Gentlemen of Verona, "love will creep in service where it cannot go." The idea that Bacon could have copied it is scornfully repulsed, though it is admitted that the play was written much earlier than Bacon's use of it; this however is accounted for by the transparent sophism, that as the play was not published until 1623, Bacon could not have obtained the phrase from that source. The fallacy of this is shown by facts accessible to any inquirer; the play in which this passage occurs was originally produced in 1591, and, as we now have it revised by Shakespeare, in 1595; it had been performed many times, and is named in a book called Wits Treasury, published in 1598, in which the following language is used in connection with it and others of Shakespeare's works, "As the soul of Euphorbus was thought to live in Pythagoras, so the great witty soul of Ovid lives in mellifluous and honey-tongued Shakespeare." No one will believe that Bacon, who was continually, as one writer says, "hanging about the court," never witnessed a court performance of any of these plays, that he never heard of the ballads that were printed about them, or of the surreptitious issues of them that were quite numerous. The truth is, he could have had no seclusion, short of solitary confinement, that could have prevented his contact with them; they were an active feature of the life of the community, and the fact of the notes in Promus containing a larger number of quotations from them than from any other source, proves Bacon's acquiescence in the popular opinion of the day; that he recognized the depth of Shakespeare's wit and sense, from their hold upon the people; and the extracts from this source, are additional evidence of his ability to discern, as well as his readiness to accept, whatever might be of use, no matter what its source. The borrowing from Shakespeare would be among the least discreditable things he ever did.

Pertinent to this phase of the discussion is a matter before alluded to. This book, set up as the expounder of proofs that a great poet had lived in Bacon, fails to produce that writer's versification of the 104th and other Psalms; the most reliable, and in reality the only practical illustration of his poetic genius that could be cited, does not appear. This specimen of Bacon's avowed handiwork, stamped, as we may say, with no mystic cipher, but bearing marks of "his blushing honours thick," is kept in the background. It is as though the complainant, having custody of the sole witness that has any real knowledge of the case, spirited that witness away and suppressed the only positive testimony. That the existence of such a witness is disclosed, must be a perplexing source of unrest, and one can almost hear this zealous lady exclaim, after the manner of ladies when they find facts uncomfortable, "I wish Bacon hadn't written that psalm!"

CHAPTER VIII.

What is known of Shakespeare's life — The burning of the Globe Theatre—Friendship between Lord Southampton and Shakespeare a deadly peril to Bacon—Play of Richard II. final and conclusive proof that Bacon had no connection with Shakespeare or the plays.

THE idea that but little is known of Shakespeare during his life is greatly exaggerated, and must be attributed to the natural desire to know everything concerning him. He is as well known as could be expected from the circumstances under which his life was passed. If he had written about himself, as Bacon did, the incidents of his life would have been fully known; or if he had been a politician or a courtier, more would have been known of his personal traits. But if he had possessed all of Bacon's book learning it would not have given him any prominence in the recorded history of the times while he only employed it in his profession.

A man of Shakespeare's tastes, with his conception of the beauty of truth and nobility in human nature, could hardly have found anything to attract him in the life of a court where lying was a fine art, even if he could have gained admission there. Yet that was, above all others, the place that possessed the most irresistible attraction for Bacon, from his youth to his death. Shakespeare's work proves him to have been a studious and industrious man; but it was in a field that denied him any popularity with the historians of his time, for none of them, I think, mentioned the stage.

Among the reasons urged to prove that Shakespeare was not an educated man, one is that no book known to have belonged to him can be now found; after two hundred and seventy years. The same is true of Bacon's books, however, for Spedding wonders what has become of them, as few, if any, have survived. It is hardly worth while to reply to such arguments. A man might have access to books without owning them, and things of such a perishable nature might be quickly destroyed in a fire like that of the Globe Theatre in 1613. It is not only a fair inference, but from concurrent facts, a reasonable deduction, that this fire brought about

Shakespeare's final and complete severance from the stage and play writing. Up to that time he seems to have been engaged in transactions in connection with it, and with property in the neighbourhood; and it was the play of Henry VIII. that was on the boards when the fire took place. The building was of wood, and what roof it had, of thatch; the destruction was quick and complete, and it is quite consistent with similar occurrences to assume, that with the building went its whole contents, especially as, from ballads of the time, some of the actors barely escaped. The probabilities are great, and any other supposition would be without practical grounds, that as the plays were written in conjunction with their performance, the manuscripts or acting versions were kept in the building and shared its fate, together with such books as may have belonged to the writers. This would be a serious stroke for the author, and confirm an already conceived and partially acted determination to retire. It would fully account for his not being in possession of the manuscripts at his death, although the more substantial reason, that they were the common property of the theatrical company, places beyond the reach of doubt, the theory that they were kept in the burned building and thus were lost. It would be natural that the softening influences of so many years devoted to cultivation of a refining and elevating pursuit, such as poetry, would be disturbed by the increasing corruptions of court and society life on the one side, and the rigidity and ascerbity of the growing puritanical element, which was working among the supporters of the theatre, on the other; the attractions of life in the country were heightened by contrast with the augmenting difficulties that these turmoils imposed upon a lover of peace and art, and having tasted of the pleasures of retirement, what may have been a misfortune in some respects was an opportune blessing in others; doubtless the uncertainty of profit inherent with this profession, became the more apparent, looking to the future, which to a man of Shakespeare's thrift, would be a weighty inducement to embrace such an opportunity for breaking away from uncongenial surroundings and unpromising prospects. In this turn of Shakespeare's career there is the same remarkable contrast with Bacon that develops ir every other circumstance of the lives of the two men, marking with the philosophy and sentiment of the plays, as well as with the temper and nature of the poet, the impulses and motives that guided his actions, as distinctly as in the life and career of Bacon, every feature betrays a positive divergence from all such influences. His wild ambition for place, power and show; his impecunious and reckless mode of living, and his disregard of obligations, as well as of the feelings and rights of those who endeavoured to shield and aid him. One historian, speaking of this characteristic, says, " Had he not inhabited a princely mansion on the Strand and kept a plentiful table at Gorhambury, Ben Jonson, instead of lauding him, might have censured with Hume, and Hobbes have been as niggardly of praise as Bayle. It was the possession of the Great Seal that made it fashionable to read what few could understand, pushed his works into circulation during an unlettered age, and gave him Europe for an auditory." If among his contemporaries there is any testimony of the love of a friend, or praise of a noble quality, I have not found it. His superiors held him in contempt, his equals

R

despised him and his inferiors ridiculed him. He had no element of popularity and no qualities to win esteem or confidence. His life, on his part, was a hunt after court favour, and on the part of the public a hunt after him by his creditors. Extravagance, show, debt and corruption ! He not only would not pay his debts, but he tried in the most shameless way to shuffle out of them. His mother paid many of them under protest against his extravagance and his associates. She complained of his servants (the names of more than one hundred and fifty are published), "that bloody Percy, a coach companion and a bed companion, a proud, profane, costly fellow;" another, "filthy, wasteful, knave," and the "Welshmen who swarm unfavourably." His brother Anthony was in constant trouble endeavouring to rescue him from suits and financial straits, and to arouse him to a sense of duty. In one instance, failing to induce him to perform some service for which he had received a large sum, Anthony wrote to the other party offering various lame excuses for Francis, and assured him that he would not forget to do his part which his brother "hath left softly slide from himself upon me."

In contrast with the love and affection with which Shakespeare was regarded by his fellows and all who speak of him, and his unbroken friendships with his company of players during the many years of association with them, what a record of enmities and hatreds does Bacon present!

The following incident is related by Mr. Fleay, showing how just was the esteem felt for Shakespeare by friends and acquaintances : " The Passionate Pilgrim reached a third edition and was reissued as certain amorous sonnets between Venus and Adonis, by W. Shakespeare, 'whereunto is added two love epistles' between Paris and Helen. These were stolen from Heywood's Troja Britannica of 1609. In his Apology for Actors (1612), he complains of the injury done him, as it might lead to unjust suspicion of piracy on his part, and adds, 'As I must acknowledge my lines not worthy his patronage under whom he hath published them, so the author I know much offended with Mr. Jaggard, that hath altogether unknown to him presumed to make so bold with his name.' In consequence, no doubt, of this remonstrance, Jaggard had to substitute a new title-page, from which Shakespeare's name was entirely omitted. He had allowed his name to be used in the titles of the London Prodigal in 1605, of the Yorkshire Tragedy in 1608, of the Passionate Pilgrim in 1609, and even of Sir John Oldcastle in 1600, without mumuring; but directly the interest of another demands justice at his hands he takes prompt action, and compels the piratical publisher to withdraw his name altogether." This printer was one of the firm of Blount and Jaggard who printed the folio edition eleven years later.

The same writer also mentions the following instance to show Shakespeare's independence of character: "Shakespeare's company being forbidden to act by the lord mayor because certain players in the city handled matters of divinity and state without judgment and decorum, went to the 'Cross-Keys' and played that afternoon, to the grief of the better sort, who knew they were prohibited. The mayor then committed two of the players to one of the comptors." Mr. Fleay says, "It is pleasing to find Shakespeare's company acting in so spirited a manner in defence of free thought and free speech. It would be more pleasing to be able to identify him personally as the chief leader in the movement, and this I believe he was."

This picture contradicts the idea of his being Bacon's tool, creature, or mask. It is improbable that a man of Bacon's timidity and order-loving instincts, would have any fellowship or connection with a man who had not more regard for the "better sort," and who had such strong friends among the disaffected, or who would take such a hostile attitude toward the bigoted prejudice of the community. The man that Bacon would select would not be of Shakespeare's stamp. This leads us to the only connection Bacon ever had with any of the plays. The playing of Richard II. as a part of the indictment against the Essex conspirators not only shows Shakespeare's independence of character, but Bacon's **appearance as a voluntary prosecutor** puts him in a hostile attitude toward the play, as well as the players.

I quote again from Mr. Fleay, who says, "In March, 1601, in the Essex trials, Meyric was indicted for having procured the outdated tragedy of Richard II. to be publicly acted at his own charge for the entertainment of the conspirators. From Bacon's speech (State Trials) it appears that Phillips was the manager who arranged the performance. This identifies the company as the chamberlain's, and therefore the play as Shakespeare's. It may seem strange that a play, duly licensed and published in 1597, could give offence in 1601; but the published play did not contain the deposition scene (iv. 1); the acted play of 1601 certainly did. This point is again brought forward in Southampton's trial: he calmly asked the attorney-general what he thought in his conscience they designed to do with the queen. 'The same,' replied he, 'that Henry Lancaster did with Richard II.' The examples of Richard II. and Edward II. were again quoted by the assistant judges against Southampton, while Essex in his defence urged the example of the Duke of Guise in his favour. From all of this it is clear that the subjects chosen for historical plays by Marlowe and Shakespeare were unpopular at court, but approved of by the Essex faction, and that at last the company incurred the serious displeasure of the queen. Accordingly, they did not perform at court at Christmas, 1601-2; and we find them travelling in Scotland instead."

It may seem, at first impression, that this is matter irrelevant to the issue, but in truth, the circumstances attending this trial are among the strongest proofs that Bacon was not the author of Shakespeare's plays.

Bacon's account of the play, as it was used in evidence against the conspirators, was as follows : "The afternoon before the rebellion Merrick, with a great number of others, that afterwards were all in the action, had procured to be played before them the play of deposing King Richard II. ; neither was it casual, but a play bespoke by Merrick, and not so only ; for when it was told him by one of the players that the play was old, and they should have loss in playing it, because few would come to see it, there was forty shillings extraordinary given to one of the players (Philips), and so thereupon played it was. So earnest was he to satisfy his eyes with the sight of that tragedy, which he thought soon after his lordship should bring from the stage to the state, but that God turned it upon their own heads." Bacon was offensively active at the trial in urging the treasonable bearing of this play as evidence of the designs of the conspirators. Sir Gilly

Meyrick's trial took place a few days after Southampton's. Southampton, who was Essex's closest friend during all these troubles, and was general of the horse under him in the Irish campaign, was Shakespeare's patron, to whom he had dedicated his Venus and Adonis and Lucrece. Under such circumstances it was only natural that Shakespeare and his company should be found near his friends, and that they should have been present to play for the Essex faction; but his presence among them cannot be reconciled with any possibility of a bond existing between Shakespeare and Bacon, or of Bacon's having the least influence or control over him. Shakespeare's attitude at this time is singularly strong evidence that he was not Bacon's creature, for if such a relation existed, Bacon was quite at Shakespeare's mercy, and in momentary peril of an explosion that would have carried him into the dock with the other prisoners, and finally to the fate that befell Essex.

To show what an exceedingly perilous position Bacon would have been in, had he been the author of the plays, it is only necessary to say that Essex had just been condemned, and that Bacon's standing with the queen was very insecure. Spedding and all his biographers enlarge upon the disfavour against Bacon, both at court and among the people. Macaulay says the queen had begun to suspect him, and Bacon says, "She did directly charge me that I was absent that day at the Star Chamber, which was very true, but I alleged some indisposition of the body to excuse it."

What then would have been the anger of the queen if it had been suddenly discovered on the trial, that Bacon was the author of the play! It would have assumed an importance that did not attach to it as written by a man who had no political ambition or standing, and must have thrown a taint upon Bacon that no defence could remove.

To realize the effect of such a revelation in the course of these proceedings, Bacon's position, standing, character and the relation in which he stood to all the parties must be borne in mind. The surprise of a sudden discovery that this man was playing a double part, and that his real character was so different from his assumed one, would have thrown the court into a state of consternation, drawn attention from the prisoners and turned it upon the attorney, with a revulsion of feeling upon the part of the queen, that would have mitigated the sentence against Essex and turned upon Bacon the whole torrent of vengeance and popular resentment.

To understand the bearing this play had upon the exciting occurrences of that period, it must be known that Pope Clement VIII. in the year 1596, issued a bull inciting the deposition of Queen Elizabeth, and it was the recital in this play, of a scene representing the deposition of Richard II. that made its production a basis for treasonable accusation and a mortal insult to the queen; rendering every one connected with it liable to a serious penalty, with the example fresh in memory, of Hayward, who had been imprisoned for a like offence. The performance of the play in the face of this condition of political affairs, shows not only the close relation that existed between Essex, Southampton and the players, but the steadfast and faithful regard of these people for the man who had been for years their constant friend and patron, and who now commanded their service, through an attachment stronger than fear of personal danger. Against these forces Bacon had voluntarily arrayed himself; for it must be remembered, he was not acting under compulsion of official position, or any necessity.

He was not obliged to appear against the prisoners. Hume says, "The most remarkable circumstance in the Essex trial was Bacon's appearance against him. He was none of the crown lawyers, so was not obliged by his office to assist at this trial; yet he did not scruple, in order to obtain the queen's favour, to be active in bereaving of life his friend and patron, whose generosity he had often experienced."

Macaulay says, "What course was Bacon to take? This was one of those conjunctures which show what men are. To a high-minded man, wealth, power, court favour, even personal safety, would have appeared of no account when opposed to friendship, gratitude and honour. Such a man would have stood by the side of Essex at the trial, would have spent all his power, might, authority and amity in soliciting a mitigation of the sentence, would have been a daily visitor at the cell, would have received the last injunctions and the last embraces on the scaffold, would have employed all the powers of his intellect to guard from insult the fame of his generous though erring friend. Bacon did not even preserve neutrality. He appeared as counsel for the prosecution. In that situation he did not confine himself to what would have been amply sufficient to prove a verdict. He employed all his wit, rhetoric and his learning, not to insure a conviction—for the circumstances were such that a conviction was inevitable—but to deprive the unhappy prisoner of all those excuses which, though legally of no value, yet tended to diminish the moral guilt of the crime, and which therefore, though they could not justify the peers in pronouncing an acquittal, might incline the queen to grant a pardon."

These extracts are given to show the glaring inconsistency of Bacon's attitude in these trials, with any theory of his connection with the play, which was a part of the indictment, drawn undoubtedly with the assistance of Bacon, if not entirely by his hand.

Macaulay furnishes a powerful plea for Bacon's absence, had he simply desired to show gratitude to his benefactor in recognition of favours received, but this is feeble compared with the plea of danger to his personal safety, had be been in the position of author of the subject of the indictment.

Whatever may be the estimate of Bacon's intellectual powers, there will be no assertion that he possessed any of the quality that makes rebels, martyrs or heroes; of the moral courage that stands up for a right, or the boldness and hardihood that faces danger in the perpetration of a wrong. If this opinion needs any support I again quote Mr. Macaulay, who says, "He seems to have been incapable of feeling strong affection, of facing great dangers, of making great sacrifices; his desires were set on things below." His historian, Joseph Devey, M.A., says, "In 1593 he sat for Middlesex and delivered his maiden speech in favour of law reform. The praises which followed so intoxicated him that in an ensuing debate on the subsidy he broke out into a flaming oration against the court, denouncing the claim as extravagant, and dwelling with pathetic sympathy upon the miseries which such exactions must cause among the country gentry, who would be constrained to sell their plate and brass pans to meet the demands of the crown.

Bacon carried his motion for an inquiry, and struck all the courtiers with horror and amazement. The queen, highly incensed, desired it to be intimated to the delinquent that he must never more expect favour or promotion. The spirit of the rising patriot was cowed; with bated breath he whispered expressions of repentance and amendment, and never afterwards played the patriot further than was consistent with his interest at court."

After this exposition of the facts of the case, and the character of the man, no one susceptible to reason, or to truth, will adhere to the opinion that a being so weak in manly traits as to fear the name of author of the plays, would courageously hazard position, and even life, upon confidence in the faithful preservation of his secret, by one who through every tie of honour, affection and self-interest, was allied to and in close sympathy with this man's victims; who was himself a sharer in their perils, and who, at any moment, might utter the word that would precipitate him to ruin.

Had there been any connection between Bacon and Shakespeare, the part Bacon had just enacted toward Essex would have suggested to his mind, a thousand fears that fate might repay him with like treachery.

The claim that Bacon was the author of Richard II. involves the heinous imputation, that as volunteer prosecutor, he eagerly and ruthlessly pursued upon a deadly charge, the men to whom, as author, he had supplied the incitement and material for their crime. It is not the friends of Shakespeare who allege this atrocity, and it is therefore evident that Bacon needs stronger defence against his mad supporters, than Shakespeare does.

A special reference here to the poems of Venus and Adonis, and Lucrece, will bring out more conspicuously the strength and duration of the bond between Southampton and Shakespeare, and the consequent peril to Bacon had he been the author. Venus and Adonis was published April 18th, 1593, and evidently was the product of leisure hours in 1592, when the theatres were closed on account of the plague. It was published by a printer of Stratford—which alone would be conclusive testimony as to Shakespeare's independent control of it—and licensed by the Archbishop of Canterbury. It reached several editions in the course of a few years, and the copyright, which from the extent of sale must have had considerable value, changed hands several times during that time; the work of printing also was done by different successors to the original printer, a feature again significant as regards non-concealment of authorship. The poem was dedicated to Lord Southampton in the following terms:

"To the
"RIGHT HONOURABLE HENRY WRIOTHESLEY,
"Earl of Southampton and Baron of Titchfield,
"Right Honourable,
"I know not how I shall offend in dedicating my unpolished lines to your lordship, nor how the world will censure me for choosing so strong a prop to support so weak a burden; only if your honour seem but pleased, I account myself highly praised, and vow to take advantage of all idle hours till I have honoured you with some graver labour. But if the first heir of my invention proved deformed, I shall be sorry it had so noble a godfather, and never after ear so barren a land, for fear it yield me still so bad a harvest. I leave it to your honourable survey, and your honour to your heart's content; which I wish may always answer your own wish, and the world's hopeful expectation.

"Your Honour's in all duty,
"WILLIAM SHAKESPEARE."

On May 9th of the following year, 1594, the poem of Lucrece appeared; it was from the same press, which then apparently changed hands; it also went through several editions spread over several years, and was dedicated as follows :

"To the
"RIGHT HONOURABLE HENRY WRIOTHESLEY,
"Earl of Southampton and Baron of Titchfield,
"The love I dedicate to your lordship is without end; whereof this pamphlet, without beginning, is but a superfluous moiety. The warrant I have of your honourable disposition, not the worth of my untutored lines, makes it assured of acceptance. What I have done is yours; what I have to do is yours; being part in all love devoted yours. Were my worth greater, my duty would show greater; meantime, as it is, it is bound to your lordship, to whom I wish long life still strengthened with happiness.
"Your Lordship's in all duty,
"WILLIAM SHAKESPEARE."

Lucrece is without doubt a part of the future "graver labour" promised in the dedication of the first poem, and exhibits the fealty of Shakespeare, as well as the loving devotion of his muse.

The facts as to the dedication and the publication under the auspices and direction of Shakespeare, have never been denied, so far as I am aware, but the authorship has been claimed for Bacon, and for the most obvious of reasons; that the claim, to have any

s

appearance of validity, must embrace everything that appeared in connection with Shakespeare's name; as, to admit that he did or could write any one of the pieces, would be to admit that he might have written them all, and that would be fatal to the whole Baconian theory. This is the plainest logic, and hardest to controvert, of all truth.

The style of these compositions, though somewhat crude, as would be natural to these "first heirs to his invention" is quite in harmony with all Shakespeare's writings; the subjects, treatment and diction, are closely comparable with the plays and especially with the work of the sonnets, given to the public in 1609. These were understood to have been written originally for private circulation among friends; from internal evidence they were begun as early as 1594, the year of the dedication of Lucrece; a great number of them are clearly addressed to Lord Southampton, and depict known events in his life; they give the fullest evidence of the continuous devoted loyalty of Shakespeare to his noble patron, which, as said in the dedication to Lucrece, "is without end," and it will be observed is carried over and far beyond the period of the trials.

The extremes of contrast are reached, when the mind reverts from this picture of undying gratitude and unfaltering devotion, to that of Bacon's unblushing treachery. Shakespeare's immortal verse is a fit embellishment of this point.

"Freeze, freeze, thou bitter sky,
That dost not bite so nigh,
As benefits forgot:
Though thou the waters warp,
Thy sting is not so sharp
As friend remember'd not."

CHAPTER IX.

Further defence of the Baconite claim impossible—Reasons for belief in Shakespeare—Ben Jonson's sketch of Shakespeare—Record proving authenticity and genuine work of the first editors—The man who stood near the king.

IN the preceding chapters it has been shown, by citations from the works of Bacon, that he had not a vestige of the genius and temper indispensable to the imagery of the plays; by a review of some of the leading features of his life and actions, that he was devoid of the sentiment that inspires their ideal of love, and that he was without the warm and manly impulses animating the pen of Shakespeare wherever virtue is extolled or vice censured, honesty and courage portrayed, or folly ridiculed. In the last chapter the wretched fallacy of the Baconite pretension is clearly exposed and the final blow given to the imposture. If, in the face of this, a belief in that palpable absurdity is still defended, it must be by those only whose credulity is stronger than reason—whose fondness for the marvellous is greater than the relish for fact, or whose density is their most prominent trait. No fact exists to support the claim; no probability can be founded upon any of the facts that do exist in connection with either of the names.

The subject might close here, but it is proper to give a slight sketch of facts and reasons that establish Shakespeare's title to the writings: The first of these is his recognized connection with them and established reputation as their author, during his whole lifetime, and in the succeeding generations with which that period was connected by living observers, who have, from their personal knowledge of the man and his works, made authentic record of the fact ; the poems of Venus and Adonis, Lucrece, and the Sonnets, bearing unmistakable impress of the same mind, known to have been written and published by him, and openly dedicated as a token of regard, to the man who was well known to be his friend and patron ; the surreptitious publication of some of the plays and the piratical use of his name, by publishers, to extend the sale of pieces that he did not write, establishing the fact that as a writer he was widely known and had a popular and creditable reputation; the rivalry and jealousy of other writers of his day, and the publicity of his work, which would have made it impracticable to maintain so successful an imposition; the testimony of those writers and of his fellow actors and co-labourers.

No word was uttered or written by any contemporary of Shakespeare—or until over two hundred years after his death—that even hints at a disbelief in his authorship or in his ability to write the plays and the sonnets. His association with his fellow actors was most intimate and constant, and his work of revising and altering plays to suit either the requirements of the law and demands of the court, or the whims of popular taste, was unremitting. He was one of a large number of playwriters of his time, notably Sackville, Marlowe, Greene, Dekker, Ben Jonson, Rowley, Peele, Lodge, Drayton, Fletcher, Kyd, Wilkins, Wilson, Tarleton, Tourneau, Davenport, Heywood, Chapman, and Chettle, all known to each other and most of them having active intercourse together—all men of bright intelligence, of sharp wit and critical nature, whose personal instincts, as well as professional ardour, would sharpen their senses toward even a slight suspicion that might improve their own position, or damage that of a rival writer. London was, at that time, a city of only about one hundred thousand people; there were never more than five companies of actors in existence at the same period, and the nature of the profession of player, as well as the prejudice against it, tended to a close acquaintance of its members. Notwithstanding this there were active jealousies between the companies and among these writers; what was called the "war of the theatres" prevailed for a long time, and the writers satirized each other, as well as the plays they wrote, in the pieces they put upon the stage. Shakespeare wrote and worked in conjunction with a number of these men, and they nearly all made changes from the various companies to others; Shakespeare never did; he maintained to the end his connection with the original company: whatever its name under its succeeding patrons, its principal components were the same, and its organization and continuation unbroken. Only one other writer appears to have had the same steadfast attachment for one company; this was Greene, who displayed the most uncompromising hostility to Shakespeare, whom he stigmatized as an "upstart crow," a "Johannes Factotum," and his verse as "bombast." It must be remembered that at this time, owing to the infancy of the drama in England, there was no fund of plays to draw upon; the diversions were all new creations, and each company had its own writers and monopolized the performance of his plays. This, and the varying change of service upon the part of some of these writers, together with their professional antagonism, makes their assent to Shakespeare's title of author, one of its strongest proofs. Convincing as such testimony must be, it is much less emphatic than the positive declarations of some of these men who were his strongest competitors. The most conspicuous of these is "rare Ben Jonson." Jonson was a man of determined character, disputatious, and fond of contention; with all his great talent and many noble traits, arbitrary and resentful; he seems to have been the only man connected with Shakespeare's company, between whom and Shakespeare there was an estrangement. This undoubtedly arose from their connection in the production of a play in which Shakespeare acted parts that he had written, while the remainder of the play was the work of Jonson. One of his noted traits was a fearless, outspoken manner and high personal integrity. In his paragraph upon Shakespeare this trait and his motive is evident. He says, "I had not told posterity this but for their ignorance" and "*to justify mine own candour.*"

Ben Jonson's sketch in his Discoveries was, without doubt, prompted by the discussions among the theatrical people regarding Shakespeare, during the time the players were collecting the plays for publication. He writes, "I remember the players have often mentioned it as an honour to Shakespeare, that in his writing (whatsoever he penned) he never blotted out a line. My answer hath been, Would he had blotted a thousand; which they thought a malevolent speech. I had not told posterity this but for their ignorance, who chose that circumstance to commend their friend by wherein he most faulted, and to justify mine own candour; for I loved the man, and do honour his memory on this side idolatry, as much as any. He was (indeed) honest, and of an open and free nature; had an excellent phantasy, brave notions and gentle expressions; wherein he flowed with that facility, that sometimes it was necessary he should be stopped. His wit was in his own power, would the rule of it had been so too. Many times he fell into those things that could not escape laughter, as when he said in the person of Cæsar, one speaking to him, 'Cæsar, thou dost me wrong.' He replied, 'Cæsar did never wrong but with just cause,' and such like, which were ridiculous. But he redeemed his vices with his virtues. There was ever more in him to be praised than pardoned."

Jonson's criticism is worth far more for the picture it draws of Shakespeare than for its estimate of him as a poet. Of that there is now no dispute; but of the qualities that Jonson attributes to him, no one will question his competent judgment. It is in perfect accord with his opinion as expressed in many places in his Discoveries, on the subject of

criticism, composition, poetry, eloquence, etc.
His criticism is very rarely in the vein of
approval; with him very little praise seasoned
an amount of faultfinding. Nothing less than
the indisputable "brave notions," "gentle expressions" and generous nature of Shakespeare
could have drawn from him the sketch I have
quoted, or his verses in the frontispiece of the
folio of 1623. He had no cause to flatter
Shakespeare. He had vented his ill-humour
and indulged his vanity in Shakespeare's lifetime by ridiculing his plays, and although this
page was written in remembrance of the
"gentle expressions" and of Shakespeare's
bearing toward him, it could hardly be expected to accord unqualified praise in the field
of poetry, and of the pen that had laboured so
often to satirize him; but in regard to Shakespeare's character, wit, which "was his own,"
fancy and facility of speech, it was as full,
choice and enthusiastic as the most ardent
friend of Shakespeare could desire.

This testimony of one of the most noted
men who figure in the pages of English literature, leads to that of the men who, shortly after
the death of Shakespeare, collected and pub-

lished his plays, *Heminge* and *Condell.* To authenticate their connection with Shakespeare, and their ability to perform this work properly and reliably, it is only necessary to say that they were stock-actors belonging to the same company with Shakespeare, during his whole term as a writer of plays; that they were his intimate and trusted friends, doubtless part-owners in the right to the plays, and from their parts in the presentation of them, familiar with every word they contained and every circumstance of their existence. To complete this linking of facts I give a synopsis of the records, largely as they appear in Mr. Fred Gard Fleay's Life and Works of Shakespeare, which, in my investigation of this subject, has been found so uniformly in accord with facts ascertained from other and reliable data, and the matter therein so clearly set forth without confusing or extraneous comment, that it forms the most comprehensive and satisfactory detail of incident and circumstance bearing on the history of the plays, that is to be found. This valuable work contains in itself, compilations abundant to sustain Shakespeare's right.

The plague raged to such an extent in the

year 1586 that the theatres of London were closed. The companies toured the provinces and other parts. That one known as Leicester's made a trip to the Continent, from whence it returned about the beginning of 1587, and in a tour of the provinces visited Stratford, the home of Shakespeare. As the last record of this period connecting him with his native village, is found about this date; and with this company, he is shortly after found in an association that continued during his whole public career; it has been justly inferred that he either accompanied it on its departure, or arranged to do so during its visit, and then joined it at some point, whence—under the instruction of some of its members who afterwards became noted actors—dates his career as a playwright and poet. In the year 1588 *William Kempe, Thomas Pope*, and *George Bryan* were members of this company. Previous to the death of Leicester, September 4th, 1588, the company had returned to London and appeared at the "Cross Keys" in Bishopsgate Street; after his death it went under the patronage of Lord Strange, who later became Earl of Derby, and its chief actor was the noted Edward Alleyn.

? In November, 1589, the play of Love's Labour Lost was performed by this company. This play is believed to be "the earliest example left us of Shakespeare's work." This was followed, in 1590, by Love's Labour Won, or Much Ado about Nothing. In 1591 the plays of Romeo and Juliet and Two Gentlemen of Verona were undoubtedly produced, and the company performed twice before the Court. In 1592 a new theatre was opened by the company, under the chief management of Edward Alleyn, and on March 3rd the old play of Henry VI, written by Marlowe, Peele, Lodge, and Greene, was given, with new scenes by Shakespeare introducing the death of Talbot, which, according to Nash—a prominent playwriter of the day—made it the success of the season and drew audiences of ten thousand. In September, 1592, Greene died. His Groatsworth of Wit, edited by Chettle, was issued September 20th. It was in this pamphlet that he alluded to Shakespeare as "an upstart crow," "an absolute Johannes Factotum," "the only shake-scene in the country, who supposes he is well able to bombast out a blank verse." The theatre was

closed in summer on account of the plague,
but the players gave two performances at
court in December and two in January, 1593.
It now enjoyed a preference at court and
maintained this ascendancy till the final closing
of the theatres in 1642, the only interruption
being the period of the Essex trials, 1601-2.
On April 18th, 1593, Venus and Adonis was
made public by Shakespeare. "On May 6th,
1593, a precept was issued by the Lords of
the Privy Council, authorizing Lord Strange's
players, Edward Allen, *William Kempe,
Thomas Pope, John Heminges, Augustine
Philipes* and *George Brian*, to play where the
infection is not, so it be not within seven miles
from London or of the court, that they may be
in better readiness hereafter for her majesty's
service." This list of names is by no means
complete. Of this company, *William Kempe,
Thomas Pope* and *George Brian* were in the
Earl of Leicester's company, which visited
Stratford in 1587 (six years before), and with
whom Shakespeare left Stratford. Augustine
Philips was the one who arranged the play of
Richard II. for Sir Gillie Meyricke eight years
later (1601) at Essex House. *John Heminge*

is the actor mentioned in Shakespeare's will, twenty-three years after, and who, in 1623, together with *Henry Condell*, collected and published Shakespeare's plays in the first folio edition. These licensees were evidently the stockholders. Shakespeare had not yet become one. On June 1st, 1593, Marlowe, the dramatist and co-worker with Shakespeare, was killed. In September Lord Strange, by the death of his father, became Earl of Derby. In consequence of the prevalence of the plague no plays were given at court during the holidays at the close of this year.

On April 16th, 1594, the company was again bereft of its patron by the death of Lord Derby. At this time Alleyn left it, and a new patron was found in the person of the Lord Chamberlain. The names of the following players are included in the list of its members:—W. Shakespeare, R. Burbadge, *J. Heminge*, A. Phillips, *W. Kempe*, *T. Pope*, G. Bryan, *H. Condell*, W. Sly, R. Cowley, N. Tooley, J. Duke, R. Pallant, and T. Goodall. C. Beeston joined soon afterwards. The poem of Lucrece was published by Shakespeare May 9th of this year, and he also commenced the Sonnets in

this year. The company played December
26th and 28th before the queen at Greenwich,
apparently in the day time, for which *Kempe*,
Shakespeare and Burbadge were paid the
following March. They played again at court
a number of times in the winter of 1595, and
payment was made to *Heminge* and *Bryan*.
Midsummer Night's Dream is shown by ample
proofs to have been produced at this date.

1596.—The Chamberlain died, and the
players went under the patronage of his son,
Lord Hunsdon. In August the only son of
Shakespeare died. After the funeral Shakespeare returned to his lodgings in Southwark,
where a draft of a grant of arms was made
later in the year to his father, John Shakespeare. The holiday performances at court by
this company, were two at Christmas and two
each, in January and February, 1597.

1597.—Shakespeare purchased New Place,
Stratford, a freehold, and "henceforth his
designation is William Shakespeare of New
Place, Stratford, Gentleman," Lord Hunsdon
became Chamberlain, and the company of
players was again known as "the Chamberlain's
men." A surreptitious edition of Romeo and

T

Juliet was published. The usual court performances were given by these players.

1598.—Ben Jonson joined the company, and his play of Every Man in his Humour was performed, the actors being Shakespeare, Burbadge, *Phillips, Heminge, Condell, Pope,* Sly, Beeston, *Kempe,* and Duke. Mere's book was published this year, in which he lauds Shakespeare and enumerates twelve of his plays. The sonnets were concluded this year. Shakespeare was then living in the parish of St. Helen's, Bishopsgate. There were three performances at court by the company during the Christmas holidays.

1599.—Shakespeare's company left its former quarters and went to the Globe Theatre, then just completed. Ben Jonson's play of Every Man out of his Humour was here performed, but in it Shakespeare did not take a part, as he had done at the performance of Jonson's earlier play. The chief actors on this occasion were Burbadge, *Heminge,* Phillips, *Condell,* Sly, and *Pope,*—Kempe had left the company. The play was full of personalities against other players and writers. Jonson soon after left the company, and his series of satirical plays was continued at a rival establishment, the contest that ensued being known as "the war of the theatres." Shakespeare's name was pirated by the publisher of some poems and sonnets, some of which were his and the remainder by inferior authors. The court plays by this company during the holidays were three in number. The last of these—February 4th,

1600—was, from the best of evidence, the Merry Wives of Windsor, which Shakespeare wrote to gratify the queen's desire to see Falstaff in love. In August the plays of Much Ado about Nothing and 2nd Henry IV., with the humours of Sir John Falstaff, written by Master Shakespeare, were licensed. The usual court performances were given.

1601.—" In March, in the Essex trials, Meyrick was indicted 'for having procured the out-dated tragedy of Richard II. to be publicly acted at his own charge for the entertainment of the conspirators. From Bacon's speech (State Trials) it appears that Philips was the manager who arranged this performance.'" In the winter of this year these players did not perform at court, being in disgrace on account of the performance of the obnoxious play; they travelled the country and even went to Scotland, where they received the additional title of "the king's servants," and Laurence Fletcher, their manager, was made a burgess of Aberdeen.

1601.—Shakespeare, Jonson, Marston, and Chapman appear as fellow contributors in Chester's Love's Martyr; with this the stage contest between them ceased. Shakespeare's father died in September of this year.

1602.—A surreptitious issue of the Merry Wives of Windsor and of Hamlet was made this year. Shakespeare purchased 107 acres and a cottage property at Stratford. Two performances were given by the players at court.

1603.—"March 24th, Queen Elizabeth died.

"May 19th, a license was granted to L. Fletcher, W. Shakespeare, R. Burbadge, *A. Philips*, *J. Heminge*, *H. Condell*, W. Sly, R. Armin, and R. Cowley to perform stage plays, within their now usual house called the Globe or in any part of the kingdom. They are henceforth nominated the king's players. *Pope*, the actor, died this year.

1604.—" In the winter of 1603-4 Shakespeare's company gave nine different plays at court. In February, 1604, £30 were given to R. Burbadge and his men for the maintenance of himself and the rest of his company, being prohibited to present any plays publicly in or near London, by reason of great peril that might grow through the extraordinary concourse and assembly of the people to an increase of the plague, till it shall please God to settle the city in a more perfect health. From July, 1603, until March, 1604, the theatres were probably closed."

"Shakespeare's company (the king's men), like those of other companies, had an allowance for cloaks, etc., to appear at the entry of King James on the 15th of March." There were nine players who appeared in scarlet on this occasion: Shakespeare, Phillips, Fletcher, *Heminge*, Burbadge, Sly, Lorrin, *Condell*, and Cowley. In the winter of 1604-5 they acted before the court seven of Shakespeare's plays and three others.

"In August the king had a special order issued that every member of the company should attend at Somerset House, when the Spanish ambassador came to England.

"The second quarto of Hamlet was published this year, newly imprinted and enlarged to almost as much again as it was, according to the new and perfect copy."

1605.—"On May 4th Philips made his will, which was proved on the 13th. In it he leaves thirty shillings each to Shakespeare and *Condell*, and twenty shillings each to Fletcher, Armin, Cowley, Cook, and Tooley, all his fellows; to Beeston, his servant, thirty shillings; to Gilburne, his 'late apprentice,' forty shillings and clothes; to James Sandes, 'his apprentice,' forty shillings and musical instruments; to *Heminge*, Burbadge, and Sly, overseers and executors, a bowl of silver of five pounds apiece.

"October 9th Shakespeare's company performed before the mayor and corporation of Oxford, and in the winter of 1605-6, ten plays at court.

"The Yorkshire Tragedy was acted this year by Shakespeare's company, and was subsequently entered on Stationer's Register as written by William Shakespeare, but it was by 'an unscrupulous, piratic printer, who on other occasions tried to establish rights in Shakespeare's plays which were not Shakespeare's, and no weight can be assigned to his assertions.' In August King James witnessed, at Oxford, the personation by students of the three sibyls who in Macbeth prophesied to Banquo, and there is every reason to believe that this circumstance induced him to send to Shakespeare, the holograph requiring a more elaborate version of that play, which is proved to have been rendered in

1606.—" In the summer of this year 'the king's men had performed three plays before the King of Denmark and his majesty—two at Greenwich, one at Hampton Court—and at Christmas they performed at court nine plays : that on December 26th was Lear, as we have it in the quarto version. The folio is that used on the stage at the same date.' "

1607.—Shakespeare's daughter was married "to Dr. John Hall, an eminent physician of Stratford." The play of King Lear was entered on Stationer's Register. In December Shakespeare's youngest brother died, and was buried at St. Saviour's, Southwark, "with a forenoon knell of the great bell." The number of court performances by the company increased this winter to thirteen.

1608.—The record shows that Shakespeare's mother was buried at Stratford on September 9th of this year, and that on the 16th of October he stood godfather to William Walker, to whom he left a remembrance in his will, and whose given name was doubtless taken from Shakespeare's. W. Sly, the player, died this year. The court festivities at Christmas included twelve performances by the company.

1609.—A surreptitious entry of Troylus and Cressida was made in January, and in May the sonnets were published, being dedicated to Mr. W. H., who, from many allusions in the poem and incidents known of his life, is understood to be Sir William Hervey, the husband of Lord Southampton's mother. Pericles was also surreptitiously printed this year. The plague was a serious scourge in 1609, and for that reason there were no dramatic performances at court.

1610.—The chief players of the company this year are shown by casts of the plays, to be Burbadge, *Heminge*, Lorrin, Ostler, *Condell*, Underwood, Cooke, Tooley, Armin, and Eggleston. Shakespeare is supposed to have retired this year from active theatrical work, completing, with Winter's Tale and the Tempest, his contributions to its literature. He made an additional purchase of land at Stratford, in June.

1611.—The principal writers for the company at this time are shown, by the new plays produced, to have been Ben Jonson, Webster, Tourneau, Beaumont, and Fletcher, and the casts of plays show the players to have been the same as the year before, except the minor change of Robinson for Armin.

1612.—Webster published his White Devil, which, in the dedication, speaks of the "right happy and copious industry" of Shakespeare. Heywood's Apology for Actors appeared, in which he complains of Jaggard's unauthorized publication, in Shakespeare's name, of verses stolen from Heywood's Troja Britannica and affirms Shakespeare's indignation at the act, after which his name was taken off the title-page by the publisher.

1613.—Shakespeare purchased a house, with shop and yard, in the immediate vicinity of the theatre, and leased it to John Robinson, who was one of those who, in 1596, had opposed the establishment of the theatre at Blackfriars, and was also one of the witnesses to Shakespeare's will. One of the trustees for the legal estate in this property—the mortgage remaining unredeemed—was *John Heminge*. On July 29th the theatre was completely destroyed by fire. The old ballad about the fire says, "the reprobates prayed for the fool and Henry Condy (*Condell*), who were apparently the last actors who escaped."

1614.—Cooke, the actor, died in this year. The documents known as those of 1635 show that by this year all the shares in the company held by *Kempe*, *Pope*, *Bryan*, Shakespeare, Sly and Cowley had reverted to the remaining shareholders: the Burbadges, *Heminge* and *Condell*.

1615.—Shakespeare was connected with an effort to enclose some common fields at Stratford, but was in London in November and December, where letters on behalf of the corporation, in opposition to the proceedings, were sent to him; the enclosure did not take place and the matter laid over until autumn of the next year.

1615.—In September of this year the project was abandoned and "this is the last notice of Shakespeare's action in any public matter."

1616.—February 10th, his daughter Judith was married; his will was executed on March 25th, he died on April 23rd and was buried on the 25th. One of the bequests in his will reads, "and to my fellows, *John Hemynge*, Richard Burbadge, and *Henry Cundell*, twenty-six shillings eight pence a-piece, to buy them rings." These men were the surviving stockholders in the theatre burned in 1613.

In preparing this record I have not aimed to make it a full list of the known incidents relating to Shakespeare's life and work; it is far short of this. Mr. Fleay's book is a large volume on which he spent ten years, and he speaks of being yet engaged in further pursuit of the same subject. I have merely selected such items as are pertinent to the propositions advanced at the beginning of this chapter, and to the purpose of showing Shakespeare's intimate relations with his fellow players and writers; in particular, his unbroken connection, during his whole stage career, with the two men who finally put his works into shape and gave them to the world—to use their own words—"**cured and perfect of their limbs and all the rest,** absolute in their numbers, as he conceived them."

From the stated dates and incidents, it will be seen that the players adhered with a wonderful tenacity to each other and to the company, in contradistinction to the writers, who, except Shakespeare, made frequent changes, and this may be greatly owing to popularity and success through Shakespeare's work; it was undoubtedly this growing popularity that caused the bitterness of Greene's hostility and satire. He had been the popular writer of the chief company, and imagined that a province which he felt belonged to him, had been invaded by a presumptuous and dangerous rival.

The earliest names with which, by the records, Shakespeare is seen in connection, are those of Kempe, Pope and Bryan, when he joined the company of Leicester's men in 1587. Bryan's association I can trace only as far as 1597, ten years; Kempe's, till he left the company in 1599, twelve years; but Pope's continued sixteen years, until his death in 1603. The earliest mention of Phillips is 1593, he died in 1605, twelve years later, and still a member of the company, leaving in his will a souvenir to Shakespeare ; W. Sly died in 1608, after fourteen years of association ; Burbadge, who was one of the owners of the theatre, survived Shakespeare and is named in his will. The dates show the connection with *Heminge* to have endured at least twenty-three years and with *Condell* twenty-two years, which linked with their association with Kempe, Pope and Bryan, covers the whole period of Shakespeare's public career ; the duration of an average life-time. The naming of *Heminge* as trustee for the mortgaged estate, proves that he was a man of respectability and worth ; he would not have been accepted by the other side in interest, if that had not been the fact. It is evident that Shakespeare continued in friendly intercourse with all these men to the end of his life, and this presents one of the most remarkable records of friendship known, especially in a calling that naturally provokes the most extreme tests of patience and indulgence ; it is on all sides an indication of sturdy and steadfast character.

It is pleasant to think that it was the wisdom that inspired the precepts for Laertes, and the spirit of "so worthy a friend and fellow as was our Shakespeare," that prevailed in the counsels of his company and bound it together "with hoops of steel."

It is difficult to read the history of the court, the intrigues, jealousies, hatreds, plots and schemes of personal ambition, and the falsehood, suspicion and duplicity that marked all its intercourse, without an involuntary comparison between it and the bond of good will and honest comradeship, that held these men together during a lifetime of devotion to their art, and of unconscious service to futurity; if the comparison be followed to Bacon, hired to defame the memory of his benefactor, on the one side, and on the other, to the two players labouring without self-profit to do "an office for the dead," it is the limit of contrast.

Their love did not end with the poet's death. Seven years later, and over thirty years after the date of their first association with him, these two men published all they could find of his work, arranged in as perfect form as it was in their power to place it. It is reasonable to suppose that they had spent most of the time between Shakespeare's death and the date of publication, in collecting and preparing the plays.

It is probable, from Ben Jonson's allusion to the players, that all of Shakespeare's fellows joined in the work of collecting and publishing, although Heminge and Condell were the principals ; and it is in harmony with the generous nature of the dear "old player," his good comradeship and modest estimate of his own gifts, that when he left the stage he should have left his plays to those who naturally seemed to inherit them, and to whom they were valuable. Their gift of them to the world was a like noble deed.

In the effort to put the plays in their proper order, to discard what was spurious and retain the acting versions, they must have been guided largely by their memory, stage experience and familiarity with the representations, and in this respect they were the fittest men for such a work ; what they say of their "care and paine" is expressive of a great task finished, which is fully justified by the volume. The world can never repay these two generous friends of Shakespeare for their tribute to his memory. It is not likely that they will be forgotten ; but they deserve an enduring memorial that should fitly record the service they performed for mankind, when they were simply labouring to pay a debt of love.

In the memoranda of dates, the note of the burial of Shakespeare's brother Edmund, at St. Saviour's, which, with his baptism at Stratford, is the only record of his existence; reveals a phase of the poet's life prompting suggestions that grow into a picture, deeply touching and pathetic. The influence that brought these brothers, the eldest and the youngest of the house, to join hands and hearts in the struggle over one of life's most rugged paths, must have had its origin in some force more potent than mere impulse. It was a deep grief that struck Shakespeare's heart in the death of the youth who was his only son; for solace, his affections must naturally turn toward his youthful brother of nearly the same age ; that this was the secret of their union, no one can well doubt. What confidences ; what affectionate unity of fatherly and fraternal love, must have bound these two men, moving together in the obscurity of a lowly and unenvied calling; creating diversions for the gay court and the careless lower world ; looking for their reward only in the consummation of some mutual purpose. No one can paint the sorrow, that into that lonely man's soul, entered with "the forenoon knell of the great bell."

The remarkable absence, in the poets' life and writings, of any desire to obtrude his personality upon the public notice, to make a place for himself in history, and his elevation of art above personal ambition, literary rivalry or fame, are the qualities which oblige his lovers to seek outside of his own writings for aids to present him to their imagination. What was his estimate of himself, what merit he thought his work possessed, and whether he ever speculated upon its place in the literature of future ages, no one can learn by any expression from him. Unlike the rule of genius distinguished in poetry, he sang no song of himself, either of vanity, pity, or complaint. While his contemporary felicitated himself that his work, carefully embalmed in Latin, should supersede "all the systems of philosophy hitherto received or imagined," Shakespeare betrayed no consciousness that in history his life's work, in a calling held in the lowest esteem, would invest him with a fame beyond any other man of the age.

"Stage acting, in the profession of it," was in that day "disreputable." It was under the ban, subject to interruption, suppression and command of the ruling power, and existed only by indulgence. It is unquestionable that had not the plays furnished amusement for Queen Elizabeth and afterward King James, and for certain noblemen who did not sympathize with the intolerant spirit of the time, the theatres would have been entirely closed, as they were a few years later. It is notable that even more plays were given at the Christmas festivities during the reign of King James, than in that of Queen Elizabeth.

"On the 2nd of September, 1642, by order of the two houses of Parliament, the theatres were closed, as a becoming measure during the season of public calamity and impending civil war." In January, 1648, another ordinance was passed forbidding all theatrical entertainments, and directing the theatres to be rendered unserviceable. The Puritans, in their zealous determination to force all classes to become devout, declared that the acting of theatrical plays should be considered a crime and punished as such, and more than this, that even witnessing of such plays was a misdemeanour. Dramatic representations were thus entirely proscribed until the year 1656; nor indeed were they restored to favour until the accession of Charles II. in 1660" (Baldwin).

The world does not realize that, had Shakespeare's career been cast fifty years later, the domination of the puritanical spirit that closed the theatres, "during which period no plays were written," would have made it impossible to produce his works. They were not finished in the manuscript, but were largely created on the stage. How much genius for art and literature has perished under a like austere influence, no one can ever know. It is impossible to name a man in thirteen hundred years of history, who sought to teach progress in liberal art, science or humanity, who did not find in that same opponent his enemy and persecutor. In Shakespeare's time there was no field in which his genius could find expression except on the stage; and it is singular that the pastimes and amusements of the most self-indulgent sovereigns should have afforded a permit, or it might be said granted a license, by which the richest jewels of poetry could have birth in an age of bitter intolerance. The testimony of the history of the time is conclusive that the theatres existed by favour and protection of the court. During the time of Cromwell they were closed. A case which illustrates the attack of the ultra sectarians upon the court, for its encouragement of the theatres, is that of William Prynne. In 1633 he published a violent attack upon the immoralities of the stage, and asserted in it that kings and emperors who had favoured the drama had been carried off by violent deaths; he also applied a disgraceful epithet to actresses. Just at that time the queen (who was very fond of dramatic entertainments) was taking part in the rehearsal of a ballet, and the offensive words were supposed to apply to her. Prynne was sentenced by the Star Chamber, put in the pillory and had his ears cut off. Prynne's offence was in the reign of Charles I.

No more absurd reason for the supposed concealment of dramatic genius could be concocted, than that it would prejudice the court against the claimant for royal favour. If this had been in Cromwell's time such a theory might have answered the purpose, but it is utterly inapplicable to the reigns of Elizabeth and James I. It was purely through their favour that Shakespeare existed as a player and dramatic poet.

The picture most attractive to imagination in the history of the court of that day, is that of those amusements and festivities in which, for the moment, it ceased from and forgot its dreadful business of government.

By the court's recognition of the stage, and its friendly protection and encouragement of the theatrical companies (whatever the motive), Shakespeare was permitted to produce his plays ; and the man who stood in the crowd at the entry of King James, clad in a cloak furnished by the government, has shed a glory upon the history of that period, and invested its principal personages with an interest, far more attractive than any that attaches to their control of its political events.

THE LEADENHALL PRESS,
LONDON, E.C.
T 4.354.

Now if you want some volumes nice,
You'll start at once I'm su-er,
And go and fetch them in a trice,
From Messrs. FIELD AND TUER.—*Punch.*

EXTRACTS FROM
Field & Tuer's List,
The ✦ Leadenhall ✦ Press,
50, *LEADENHALL STREET, E.C.*

Upwards of 300 Superb Illustrations (some beautifully hand-coloured).

KENSINGTON: PICTURESQUE AND HISTORICAL. By W. J. LOFTIE, B.A., F.S.A., Author of "A History of London," &c., &c. Illustrated by W. LUKER, JUN., from Original Drawings carefully finished on the spot and engraved in Paris. LONDON: Field & Tuer, The Leadenhall Press, E.C. £2 5s.

Since the publication of Faulkner's work in 1820, no history of Kensington pretending to accuracy or completeness has been produced. This sumptuous work contains full and descriptive accounts of the parish of Kensington and the adjoining Palace and Gardens, with the changes and improvements of the past half century or more; notices of Kensington celebrities and of the great national institutions which have sprung up at Kensington Gore and Brompton Park; and a fund of discursive matter of local and historical interest. In regard to the very numerous and absolutely faithful illustrations, two years have been spent by the artist in making for this work original drawings of old and modern Kensington. They include artistic exteriors and interiors; glimpses of Kensington Gardens; the Palace in which the Queen was born; the park; the people, streets, houses, churches, and ruins; and pretty, quaint, and taking "bits" of Kensington scenery. All the drawings have been engraved in Paris in the finest possible manner, and the paper on which they are printed has been specially manufactured of a quality to ensure the delicacy of the originals being fully retained.

For the curious a few PROOF copies of KENSINGTON: PICTURESQUE AND HISTORICAL at five guineas, bound in full morocco, have painted in water-colours on the front, under the gilt edges of the leaves, a couple of Kensington views, which, until the leaves are bent back at an angle, are invisible.

THROUGH ENGLAND ON A SIDE-SADDLE IN THE TIME OF WILLIAM & MARY; being the Diary of CELIA FIENNES. With an explanatory Introduction by The Hon. Mrs. GRIFFITHS. LONDON: Field & Tuer, The Leadenhall Press, E.C.

TALES FROM THE LANDS OF NUTS & GRAPES: (SPANISH & PORTUGUESE FOLKLORE.) By CHARLES SELLERS. LONDON: Field & Tuer, The Leadenhall Press, E.C.
[Half-a-Crown.

THE BAIRNS' ANNUAL (for 1888-9) of Old-Fashioned Tales. Edited by ALICE CORKRAN. Illustrated with nearly one hundred original wooden blocks and a coloured Frontispiece. Contents:—The Story of Punch and Judy: The Sleeping Beauty in the Wood: The Butterfly's Ball and the Grasshopper's Feast: Little Red Riding Hood: Hop o' my Thumb: Cinderella and her Little Glass Slipper: Gaffer Gray: a Christmas Ditty: The Apple-Pie Alphabet: Dr. Watts's Cradle Hymn: Peter Piper's Practical Principles: A Merry New Song: The Rudiments of Grammar: The Froward Child Properly Corrected: Tom Thumb. LONDON: Field & Tuer, The Leadenhall Press, E.C. [One Shilling. A delightful *mélange* of the old-fashioned fairy tales that delighted our grand-parents when bairns.

MEN, MAIDENS & MANNERS A HUNDRED YEARS AGO. By JOHN ASHTON. With thirty-four contemporary illustrations. LONDON: Field & Tuer, The Leadenhall Press, E.C. [One Shilling.

HIEROGLYPHIC BIBLE. Being a careful selection of the most interesting and important passages in the Old and New Testaments. Illustrated with hundreds of Engravings on Wood. LONDON: Field & Tuer, The Leadenhall Press, E,C. [One Shilling. A facsimile, crowded with the original quaint illustrations, of an edition of the Holy Scriptures which amused and instructed our great grand-fathers and great grand-mothers when little boys and girls.

A LOVER'S LITANIES. By ERIC MACKAY, Author of "Love Letters of a Violinist" and "Gladys the Singer." LONDON: Field & Tuer, The Leadenhall Press, London, E.C. [Ten-and-Sixpence.

THE BAGLIONI: A Tragedy. By FAIRFAX L. CARTWRIGHT. LONDON: Field & Tuer, The Leadenhall Press, E.C.
[Three-and-Sixpence.

PEOPLE WE MEET. By CHARLES F. RIDEAL. Illustrated by HARRY PARKES. LONDON: Field & Tuer, The Leadenhall Press, E.C.
[One Shilling.
A limited edition of 250 only, proof copies signed and numbered.
[Five Shillings.

THE GRIEVANCES BETWEEN AUTHORS AND PUBLISHERS, being the Report of the Conferences of the Incorporated Society of Authors held in Willis's Rooms, in March, 1887. with Additional Matter and Summary. LONDON: Field & Tuer, The Leadenhall Press, E.C. [Two Shillings.

www.ingramcontent.com/pod-product-compliance
Lightning Source LLC
Chambersburg PA
CBHW022109230426
43672CB00008B/1326